UNDERSTANDING
CHINA
IN THE NEW ERA

Li Wen

Long River Press
San Francisco

Published in the United States of America by

Sinomedia International Group

Long River Press

360 Swift Avenue, Suite 48

South San Francisco, CA 94080

www.chinabooks.com

ISBN 978-1-59265-229-7

Author: *Li Wen*

Text and cover design: *Kana Barker*

Special thanks: *Huang Youyi*

CONTENTS

CHAPTER I

SETTING THE COURSE FOR THE FUTURE

—Understanding the 19th National Congress of the Communist Party of China

In October 2017, during the early autumn of Beijing, the Communist Party of China (CPC) held its 19th National Congress. The widely anticipated conference was attended by over 2,300 delegates from different parts of the country, who convened in the Great Hall of the People where General Secretary Xi Jinping delivered his report on reaching the goal of a moderately prosperous society, and pursuing socialism with Chinese characteristics in a new era. United in their resolve to achieve national renewal, the delegates deliberated on important issues for the future development of both the CPC and the nation. The event drew global attention, with more than 1,000 congratulatory messages from over 450 major political parties in 160 countries and regions, and coverage by more than 1,800 reporters from 130 countries.

The 19th CPC National Congress marks a new chapter in Chinese history. Held at a critical time when socialism with Chinese characteristics is entering a new era, it unveiled a roadmap for realizing the dream of the people. This draws on lessons from the past, and has adjusted to the changing times, and will guide us towards national renewal.

AN IMPORTANT EVENT AT A CRITICAL TIME

Like other key milestones at critical moments in history that set a course for the path forward, the 19th National Congress, an important conference held at a critical juncture, provides guidance for the CPC and the nation in a new journey towards a brighter future.

For any long journey, there are always a few critical junctures. Looking back, we are proud of our achievements against heavy odds since the founding of the People's Republic of China (PRC) in 1949, and especially since the launch of the reform agenda in 1978. The Chinese nation has taken great strides forward from the earliest days of the new republic, through rising prosperity and to its present strong standing in the international community.

Extensive coverage by Chinese and foreign media
As the 19th CPC National Congress proceeds, it is covered by Chinese and foreign press through live broadcast, life reports, interviews, rolling news feed, etc.

As we embrace the prospect of national renewal, we know we are now at another critical point. Our journey forward will not be easy, but we are ready for the new challenges.

Quality tops our development agenda. China's sustained economic growth, which has amazed the world and made it the second largest economy, should not however, hide the fact that China is still -- and will remain for a long time -- in the primary stage of socialism, and that it is still the world's largest developing country. We must seize promising opportunities to pursue our goals, and overcome new difficulties and challenges along the way. We can no longer continue a growth strategy based on economic expansion only, for it will not take us much further. That is why an important transition is necessary to move towards a model that focuses more on quality. To this end, initiatives are needed for progress in different areas including green technology, artificial intelligence, environmental protection, etc. At the same time, more must be done to narrow the development gap between urban and rural areas, between different geographical regions, as well as the income gap between rich and poor. Major headway is needed in three areas: improved quality, better efficiency and a shift in growth drivers. These transformations are necessary for China's economy to achieve sound and sustainable growth.

China's reform is now in a critical stage. We need the courage and resolve to fight many uphill battles. Since the reforms entered a most difficult phase after the 18th CPC National Congress held in 2012, over 1,500 new measures have been implemented, and substantial progress made in crucial areas, laying the groundwork for more in-depth reforms. As these proceed and deepen, there is bound to be greater resistance: inertia and networks of vested interests will present increasingly serious challenges. But we cannot waver. We must forge ahead and overcome them, for our nation's future depends on successful reforms.

We are now at a crucial juncture in our journey towards the two Centennial Goals. The next five years, between the 19th and the 20th CPC National Congresses, will witness the realization of the First Centennial Goal of building a moderately prosperous society by 2020. Also during this period, the more ambitious process will be initiated to achieve the Second Centennial

Goal of a modern socialist country by 2049. It is, so to speak, a period when one chapter closes and a new one opens. We cannot afford to fail to reach either of these goals.

A CONFERENCE WITH A SIGNIFICANT THEME

For each of its national congresses, the CPC sets a theme that frames its deliberations, a theme that also sets the course for the CPC's future actions and development.

As China enters a new era, much international and domestic attention has focussed on the CPC. What is its guiding theory? What is its motivation? What is its mission? How will it fulfill its goals? The answers can be found in General Secretary Xi Jinping's report to the 19th National Congress, when he declared that the CPC must stay true to its original ideals and remain faithful to its mission, that is, to continue on the path of socialism with Chinese characteristics, build a moderately prosperous society in all respects, and realize the Chinese dream of national renewal.

His statement clearly enunciates the CPC's long-time commitment to this mission which members must never forget no matter how much they have achieved. For the past 97 years since its founding in 1921, the CPC has consistently worked to improve the lot of the Chinese people and to revive the Chinese nation. This same mission guided the CPC thoughout its history, whether distributing land to poor farmers in the first land reform in the 1920s, defeating the Japanese invaders in World War II, overthrowing the reactionary rule of the Kuomintang, or more recently promoting economic development and carrying out reforms. A strong country, a prosperous nation and a contented people was and still is our overarching mission, which will continue to motivate us into the future.

His statement also makes clear the CPC's commitment to socialism with Chinese characteristics. Such a theoretical framework did not simply fall from the sky. It has evolved at great cost and out of the countless hardships experienced by both the CPC and the people. It is the result of many lessons drawn from history: 40 years of reform and opening up; close to 70 years

Delegates to the 19th CPC National Congress discussing the report to the Congress.

of continuous trial and error since the founding of the People's Republic in 1949; 97 years of social revolution led by the CPC since its founding in 1921; over 170 years of change from a once weak country to a strong nation today, as well as over 5,000 years of uninterrupted civilization. It is indeed a very hard-won achievement. As the CPC sets out to fulfill its historical mission in the new era, it will continue to follow this path of socialism with Chinese characteristics.

His statement reaffirms the specific goals of the CPC: the First Centenary Goal to build a moderately prosperous society in all respects by 2020 is only two years away, and the charge has been launched. We must make one final push for complete victory. Then we will continue on to the Second Centenary Goal to realize the Chinese dream of national renewal by 2049. We must call on our people's sustained efforts to build China into a strong, modern socialist country. Many past generations had this dream of national renewal, and when it is fulfilled we can be proud that we have lived up to the expectations of our predecessors.

A CONFERENCE WITH A FULL AGENDA AND IMPORTANT OUT-COMES

The 19th CPC National Congress had a packed schedule: 5 major agenda items deliberated over 7 days in presidium, plenary, and group sessions, in addition to a number of side events, including 6 press conferences, 8 group interviews, open house gatherings by 34 delegations, and "Delegates Meet the Press" opportunities. The candid and transparent discussions were lively, many interesting ideas were aired, and the final decisions reached have far reaching significance.

A new leadership was elected. Deng Xiaoping once commented on the essential role of the CPC: "To govern China well, the Party is key", and "It is essential for the Party to have a strong political bureau, particularly a strong standing committee". At the national congress, the 19th CPC Central Committee was elected which in turn elected, a new central leading group with Xi Jinping at its center. With a new leading body that consists of people

Delegates meeting the press

The Media Center of the 19th CPC National Congress set up a space in the hall-way leading to the main conference room for delegates to meet the press so that reporters had more opportunities to interview and engage with delegates up-close. This was the first time for such an arrangement at a CPC national congress. Sixty delegates met the press and answered questions. Above: three delegates are interviewed by Chinese and international reporters.

who have the experience, capability and credibility, the CPC stands ready to provide the strong political leadership needed for both the CPC's growth and national development in the new era. The elections drew enthusiastic applause, demonstrating both support and confidence.

New times require new thinking and guidance. This has been effectuated by including the concept of Xi Jinping Thought on Socialism with Chinese Characteristics for a New Era in the revised Constitution of the CPC, thus laying out a new theoretical framework and roadmap for the new era in response to the changing times. The course for future action is now clear. Herein lies the primary significance of the 19th CPC National Congress: application of Marxism to the Chinese context in the 21st century.

New goals were adopted and specific measures were decided on at the 19th CPC National Congress. A good understanding of China's present situation is needed as a reference point to chart a course for socialism with Chinese characteristics in the new era. This underpins everything the CPC should do from now on. Based on its understanding of where the country is in its historical development and its specific needs at this stage, the CPC made a number of political assessments and laid out strategies for China's modernization over the next three decades.

A WeChat public account used for the first time for the 19th CPC National Congress

For instance, in this new era, our focus is how to meet people's growing demand for a better life while development is still uneven and insufficient; another goal is building a moderately prosperous society in the next few years, and passing through two phases to transform China into a strong and modern socialist country. We now have a new starting point and clear road-map for the future.

Specific dispositions for future work in many areas were laid out. With theory, goals and roadmap in place, planning and work will now focus on upgrading the economy, strengthening people-centered governance institutions, fostering socialist cultural values, raising people's living standards and providing better social guarantees, improving the natural environment, modernizing national defense and the armed forces, working towards national reunification within the framework of "One Country, Two Systems", enhancing the CPC's ability to lead and govern, and building an international community of shared future. Provincial authorities, central government agencies and different sectors now know clearly what they need to do.

At its second plenary session held on January 18 and 19, 2018, the newly elected Central Committee adopted recommendations on amendments to the Chinese Constitution, which, among other things, proposed to include in the Constitution some of the theories, practices and systems developed over recent years, as well as major guidelines and principles set forth during the Congress, in particular Xi Jinping Thought on Socialism with Chinese Characteristics for a New Era. It was an act needed for the cause of the Party and the country's future development. With these amendments, the Constitution provides full legal backing to socialism with Chinese characteristics, and to achieving the two "Centennial Goals" for national renewal.

TWO CONTINUOUS REVOLUTIONS

During a press conference on October 25, 2017 after the election of members of the Standing Committee of the Political Bureau, General Secretary Xi Jinping said categorically, "There is ample evidence that the CPC is capable of leading the Chinese people in a great social revolution, and is also fully able to transform itself in a self-revolution."

Some two months later on January 5, 2018, Xi Jinping elaborated on these two revolutions in his opening remarks at a seminar on implementing the principles of the 19th CPC National Congress. He stressed the importance of consolidating socialism with Chinese characteristics, of Party-building, and of being more aware and prepared for difficulties, dangers and risks. Ninety-seven years of struggle and experience have taught the CPC that strict Party discipline is essential for building a modern socialist country.

Social revolution is the fundamental political goal of the CPC. For nearly a century since its founding in 1921, the CPC has never wavered from this goal, whether through revolution, economic development or reforms. In the process, it has achieved many extraordinary things. Today, socialism with

Chinese characteristics is the continuation of this social revolution. Ancient and recent history have taught us that any radical social change would require time. Therefore, we must continue to forge ahead to secure victory in this new era, and demonstrate the strength and appeal of socialism with Chinese characteristics.

One of the most outstanding qualities of the CPC is its capacity to change from within and instill strict self-discipline. For nearly a hundred years, it has remained strong not because it has made no mistakes, but because it has been able, with the support of the people, to recognize and rectify them from within. In the new era, it must continue to build on this capacity for self-revolution to become stronger and more effective. This is necessary not only for it to continue to lead China's social transformation, but also for its own future as a political party guided by Marxism. The CPC's continued vitality depends on this self-revolution and the complete fulfillment by its ranking members of the requirements for political conviction, commitment, accountability, competency and ethics.

Social revolution and self-revolution are closely connected. In the last five years since its 18th National Congress, the CPC has worked on both. On the one hand, it has deepened reforms, overcome entrenched institutional problems, resolved complex developmental issues, and succeeded in releasing enormous social vitality which has won widespread public approval and support. On the other, it has focused on strict internal Party governance to deal with the most widely criticised issues that undermine the CPC's leadership, thus initiating a new phase in Party-building. It is fair to say that the historic achievements and changes since the 18th National Congress are all the result of this close connection between social and self-revolution.

The times set the test; CPC members take the test and the people are the graders. Yesterdays' successes are no guarantee of future ones, and the same applies to past glories. CPC members are revolutionaries who must not lose their revolutionary spirit. For the Party and nation to flourish, for peace and order to prevail, we must retain the energy and enthusiasm of the revolutionary war years. Victories and achievements are no reason for arrogance or complacency, challenges are no reason for pulling back. We must continue on with the two revolutions so that we can provide good answers to the test.

History marches on. Events occurring at crucial junctures influence the direction it takes. We are standing at a point where the past and the future meet, where China and the world converge. The 19th CPC National Congress opens a new and important chapter in the revival of the Chinese nation and is a contribution to the development of world peace and human progress.

Five Requirements for Ranking Party and Government Officials

On January 5th, 2018, in his opening remarks at a seminar on the implementation of the principles of the 19th CPC National Congress, General Secretary Xi Jinping talked about the need for members of the CPC Central Committee as well as ministerial and provincial-level officials to fulfill requirements in five areas.

They must have strong political conviction to be steadfast believers in and true practitioners of the broad ideals of communism, and of socialism with Chinese characteristics.

They must have strong political commitment to the cause of the CPC, to its larger and long-term goals, to its core leadership and to the guidelines and principles set by the CPC Central Committee. They must remain unwavering in their political stance, and be aware of their political direction, principles and path. They must protect the CPC's authority, implement its political guideline and strictly observe its discipline and rules.

They must have a strong sense of responsibility. As they perform their duties, they should be down-to-earth, and work to fulfill their responsibility for the people, instead of trying to build their own political assets and career ambitions.

They must be competent. They must have the ability to learn and expand their horizons, and to improve all round leadership skills.

They must have a proper leadership style. They must keep the people's interests at heart at all times, to listen to them, learn from them, accept their oversight and serve them well. In the performance of these duties, they must maintain a high level of political commitment and ensure that decisions are made on the basis of solid study and research. They must enrich their ideas and experiences to become competent leaders in their respective field. They must be able to learn from mistakes, regularly reflect on the work and apply theories to their work at hand, in a process of self-cultivation and improvement. They must also make consistent efforts to fight wrong ideas and behaviors, such as form over substance, excessive bureaucratic practices, pleasure-seeking, and extravagance.

CHAPTER 2

USHERING IN THE NEW ERA

—Understanding new realities and evolving challenges

At 11:05 am on June 26, 2017, two "Fuxing Hao" ("Rejuvenation") bullet trains pulled out of Beijing and Shanghai from opposite ends of the high-speed railroad linking the two metropolises. As the super fast trains sped through the land at a record-setting 350 kilometers per hour, they created another engineering marvel for the country. Deploying a full range of Chinese technologies, they embody the Chinese people's hopes for a better life and for national renewal. This is in sync with our march towards a better future in a new era of socialism with Chinese characteristics.

The journey towards national renewal is going to be long, and today we are setting out from a new starting point. With a thorough assessment of development and reform at their current stage, the 19th CPC National Congress made a critical decision to steer China into a new era of socialism with Chinese characteristics. It is an important decision that charts a new path for China.

SOCIALISM WITH CHINESE CHARACTERISTICS IN A NEW ERA

The arrival of the new era was greeted with enthusiasm on social media as circles of friends were buzzing with excitement: "The new era is so cool!" "A new era, a stronger China," and "A new era, a better life." …

There is an old Chinese saying that emphasizes the importance of understanding the general context one is in. Our historical context today is that socialism with Chinese characteristics is now in a new era. Such an assessment is not conjured out of thin air but has sound theoretical and empirical bases, both historical and contemporary. These are: important progress achieved by the Chinese people through arduous struggle under the CPC leadership; major changes in social challenges; new requirments for fulfilling the CPC's goals; and a new international environment. The report to the 19th CPC National

Congress offers an in-depth examination of the historical and political significance of this assessment from both practical and theoretical perspectives, and from a Chinese as well as an international angle. This assessment represents a new strategic starting point for building a brighter future.

The new era for national renewal is of great importance to the Chinese nation. Our modern history has been filled with turmoil and wars, Western intrusion by gunboat policy, territorial fragmentation, and widespread poverty and suffering. It was the CPC that led the Chinese people in a long and arduous revolutionary struggle to walk out of this dark period, and it continues to lead the nation with trailblazing and innovative strategies to reform and develop. We have progressed from poverty through greater prosperity and now towards national strength. We can stand tall, be confident and proud as never before.

The new era is an important time for China as it stands firm as a convincing example of scientific socialism in the world. Socialism as a concept first appeared about 500 years ago. It evolved from utopian to scientific socialism, went from theory to practice, spread from one country to many, and experienced many ups and downs. As the world socialist movement fell to its low point in the beginning of the 1990s, there was growing pessimism about the prospect of socialism, and doubts about its viability in China. Now after more than two decades, however, the Chinese model exhibits more dynamism than ever, injecting new life into the continuing cause of scientific socialism.

This is also a time for China to share with the rest of the world its unique approach to addressing issues facing mankind. Modernization is an important sign of progress, and all nations strive for it, especially developing countries. China's path to modernization is very different from that followed by Western nations. Since the founding of the PRC in 1949, especially since the launch of the reform and opening up policy in the 1980s, China's unique socialist approach has shown increasing promise. We have growing confidence in the path we have chosen, in the theories that guide us, in the political system we follow and in our cultural heritage. Facts have shown that there is more than one path to modernization. The Chinese model offers an alternative for those countries and peoples that wish to grow at a faster pace while maintaining their independence.

WHAT IS MEANT BY THE NEW ERA?

In 2017, Meridian Line Films, a UK-based film studio, made a three-episode documentary *China: Time of Xi,* which was shown on the US Discovery Channel in mid-October that year. It introduced international audiences to the great changes that had taken place in China over the past five years. The show generated widespread interest in China's new era.

So what is new about it?

First, it is a new chapter in China's development, to be followed by many other chapters. It is the cumulative result of 97 years of hard struggle and change on the part of the Chinese people under the leadership of the CPC. Development has been especially remarkable since the rollout of the reform agenda, starting in 1978, when the CPC began to lead the way in pursuing a distinctly Chinese approach to socialist development. The resulting unprecedented economic growth has enabled China to catch up with global development, and is proving socialism's relevance in a Chinese context. We stand at a new starting point today, and must continue to build on what we have achieved. This is the responsibility history has placed on this generation of CPC members, and we must not shrink from it.

Second, it is a new strategy for growth. Since early modern times the Chinese people have been striving to build a strong and modern country. World history shows that it took about 300 years for a country or region to complete its process of modernization. We are aiming to complete the same process within 100 years. This will entail a faster pace of change in all aspects of social and economic life. There is no doubt about the huge challenges ahead. After examining today's realities and future trends, the 19th CPC National Congress laid out a strategic roadmap that will guide us in achieving the goal of building a moderately prosperous society by 2020, and then continuing to build China into a strong, modern socialist country by mid-century. The call to action has been sounded, and we will be marching to a new rhythm in this new era.

Third, it is new aspirations for a better life. Improving the lot of the people has always been the driving motivation for the CPC. The years of revolution, the massive rebuilding programs and reform initiatives have all been to improve the lives of the people. Thanks to sustained efforts there has been a steady improvement in living standards. With that comes new expectations. In response to the increasingly diverse needs of our citizens, the 19th CPC National Congress unveiled a series of measures aimed at further improving popular wellbeing, enhancing social equity and justice, and creating a more satisfying, happier and safer environment.

Fourth, it offers an opportunity for us to fulfill the dream of national renewal, which has inspired so many Chinese since the Opium Wars in the mid-19th century. This is a long journey that will require passing the torch through several generations. The great changes that have occurred over the decades, especially since the CPC's 18th National Congress in 2012, have brought us closer than ever to realizing this dream, and today we are more confident than ever in our ability to do so. This new era presents us with brighter prospects, but there are still many obstacles and challenges to overcome. Only concerted and sustained efforts by all will make the Chinese dream come true.

Fifth, it is a time for a new role for China in the international arena. China's growing comprehensive national strength has significantly raised its profile on the world stage and given it new international influence. Today China engages with the rest of the world on a new footing. It participates in, contributes to and leads the promotion of world peace and development. In this new era, China will use its growing international influence in a constructive manner, advocate a new model of major-country relations, assume greater international responsibilities, work towards a global community of shared future, and contribute more to world peace, development and human progress.

A HISTORIC SHIFT IN MAJOR SOCIAL CONTRADICTIONS

Dialectical materialism tells us that every society is full of contradictions and some play a major role in shaping social processes. Only when we are able to identify these key contradictions, can we devise effective strategies to solve problems, increase forward momentum and expand opportunities.

Once the major social challenges are dealt with effectively, other issues can be resolved with relative ease. The CPC developed policies and strategies for different periods on the basis of a careful assessment of the major opposing forces at play at the time. For example, during the Agrarian Revolution in the 1920s, the major conflict was between the CPC representing the interests of the people and the Kuomintang (KMT) reactionaries representing the interests of big landowners and the wealthy bourgeoisie. The War of Resistance against Japanese Aggression (1931-1945) was a war in which the Chinese nation fought against Japanese imperialism and invasion. During the War of Liberation (1946-1949), the overriding struggle was between the Chinese people and the KMT reactionaries supported by US imperialists. Proper identification of the defining contradictions in different periods provided a sound basis for developing corresponding strategies to defeat imperialism, feudalism and crony capitalism – often referred to as "the Three Mountains", and winning the new democratic revolution.

The year 1956 marked the end of the stage of socialist transformation and beginning of the period of developing a socialist economy. The 8th CPC National Congress concluded that the overriding issue then was how to turn a backward agrarian economy into an advanced industrialized one, and how to achieve rapid economic and cultural development. Both of these were the general aspirations of the people. At its Sixth Plenary Session held in 1981, the 11th CPC Central Committee continued in this direction by emphasizing that the most important task was to upgrade backward productive sectors to meet the people's material and intellectual needs. Thanks to this assessment, we took the appropriate steps that brought about today's prosperity.

It is always necessary to respond to new realities and developments. In this new era, production, as well as supply and demand are all changing. Based on assessments of the evolving realities, the 19th CPC National Congress came to the conclusion that our primary task today is to overcome the existing imbalances and inadequacies of development, and to satisfy the growing demands of the people for a better life. Let us look at these changing realities:

First, social demand. Meeting the basic needs of 1.3 billion people has pretty

Tourism has become an important part of people's lives. During the National Day holiday and the Mid-Autumn festival seasons in 2017, tourist sites across the country were visited by more than 700 million people.

much been achieved, and the goal of a moderately prosperous society in all respects will soon be reached in 2020. However, people desire not just affluence, but also a better quality of life: more satisfaction and happiness, a safer environment, more democracy, strengthened rule of law, and greater equity and justice. They also have increasing expectations in areas such as education, employment, income, social security, healthcare, living conditions, environmental protection, and culture.

Second, production. It has skyrocketed thanks to over 40 years of fast growth since the launch of major reform measures in 1978. In many areas, China has gone from playing catch-up to running neck and neck with frontrunners, and even to taking the lead. Today, the term "backward" can no longer be applied to China's production sectors. Instead, imbalances and inadequacies in development are the most daunting problems we face. There are serious wealth gaps between booming metropolises and remote rural areas, and between modern eastern and backward western regions of the country. While China leads the world in cutting-edge technologies such as bullet trains, supercomputers, Five-hundred-meter Aperture Spherical Radio Telescope (FAST) and mobile payment systems, many farming communities still rely on animals and old-fashioned tools to work the land, and production is still at the mercy of the elements. This development gap is the main obstacle standing in the way of a better life for all.

Times have changed and the former strategy no longer corresponds to today's realities as upgrading backward production sectors is no longer the major issue. At its 19th National Congress, the CPC made an assessment that took into account the changes and developments, and laid out what is required to respond to new demands and aspirations of the population. It provides a sound basis for better-targeted policy initiatives.

WHAT HAS CHANGED AND WHAT HAS NOT?

With all these changes, people may ask if China has already passed the primary stage of socialism, and has graduated from the ranks of developing countries. The answer can be found by looking at what has changed and what remains unchanged, and if a proper strategy could be put in place in response to the changes.

While change is a constant, there are also things that do not change. We face different challenges today, but we still have the same position as to where we are in our development, in other words, we are still in the primary stage of socialism, and China is still the largest developing country in the world. It is crucial to understand this basic reality. That is why China's fundamental policy remains unchanged: economic development is still our central task. And we remain committed to the Four Cardinal Principles and the policy of reform and opening up. In the new era, we will continue our efforts in the following areas:

Maintaining an appropriate growth rate. Though China has become the world's second largest economy, its per capita GDP is not high: only about

one seventh that of the US, ranked behind more than 60 countries. An appropriate growth rate is vital to solving many problems, and it is the key to upgrading the quality of economic development, raising its efficiency, and improving people's wellbeing. That is why economy tops the CPC's agenda for national development. Stimulating productivity will provide the sound material basis for improving the lives of our people.

Improving growth quality and efficiency. For many years, China followed an extensive economic growth model relying on large inputs and extensive use of resources. Over the long term, this is not sustainable. Instead, improved quality and efficiency will lay a solid foundation for sustained economic development. China's economy is now moving from high-growth to a focus on quality and efficiency. New thinking is needed to unleash development potential, shift major growth drivers, and boost productivity.

Coordinating development efforts. Many years of hard work have produced an economic miracle that is the envy of the world. However, issues such as development imbalances, poor coordination and inconsistencies are also rife. As a result, the benefits accrued are not universally shared. The new era is a call to action. Just as an orchestra must play together to produce beautiful music, our development drive demands an integrated approach to overcome deficiencies, narrow disparities, and coordinate development in urban and rural areas. All economic and social progress relies on this coordination.

The past is behind us, and we must look to the future. The world socialist movement has experienced numerous ups and downs over the centuries. Today it is showing great promise in China. This unique Chinese socialist model for a new era represents progress for mankind, and opens a new chapter for the world socialist movement.

The significance of a new era of socialism with Chinese characteristics

The arrival of the new era of socialism with Chinese characteristics is of great significance not only in the history of the People's Republic of China and that of the Chinese nation, but also for the development of global socialism and that of human society. It signifies:

(a) that the Chinese nation, after a long period of suffering in modern history, pulled off a great leap from an emerging republic through greater prosperity to a strong nation that is embracing the prospect of national renewal,

(b) that scientific socialism is showing great promise in 21st-century China, attracting global attention to the Chinese model of socialism; and

(c) that the distinctly Chinese approach to socialist development, supported by our guiding theories, political system and culture, represents China's contribution to addressing issues facing humanity, and provides a viable new path to modernization for developing countries, especially those that wish to accelerate the process of their modernization while protecting their independence from being encroached upon by outside interference.

Today's major challenges: imbalances and inadequacies in development

Leng Rong (Director, Office of Party Literature Research of the CPC Central Committee): As the report to the 19th CPC National Congress pointed out, chief among the many issues hindering efforts to improve the wellbeing of the people are imbalances and inadequacies in development. Gaps between geographical regions are a

25

drag on our overall national development. Inadequate growth also exists in a number of sectors and industries. These deficiencies are interrelated, creating many other problems and leading to contention. They are presently the major source of social discontent and friction. A clear understanding of the issues is essential to finding solutions.

CHAPTER 3

ACHIEVING INITIAL SUCCESSES IN THE NEW ERA

—Understanding the historic achievements and transformations since the 18th CPC National Congress

As visitors walked into the Beijing Exhibition Center, their eyes were immediately caught on replicas of the *Jiaolong* deep-sea research submersible, the C919 airliner, the Wukong Dark Matter Particle Explorer (DAMPE), and the *Liaoning* aircraft carrier. They were, among many other things, exhibits showcasing China's achievements over the past five years. The exhibition consisted of 10 display areas, using illustrations, texts, videos and 3-D models to highlight the historic achievements in all fields since the 18th CPC National Congress. The three-month event drew over 2.6 million visitors to the site, and 22 million online visitors. Many left messages in the guest books expressing their pride and delight.

Yet none of this has come easily. The five years since the 18th National Congress in 2012 have been extraordinary in the history of both the CPC and the nation. Thanks to clear guidance and strong leadership from the CPC Central Committee led by Xi Jinping, the Chinese people have worked tirelessly, overcoming daunting obstacles to make the fundamental transformations necessary for the next chapter in our development. At the 19th CPC National Congress, a full review of these great successes and changes reinforced confidence in our chosen path, political system, guiding theories and values, and served to encourage both the CPC and the people in the new era.

FIVE YEARS OF HARD WORK

On November 15, 2012, the newly elected members of the Standing Committee of the Political Bureau of the 18th CPC Central Committee met the press for the first time. General Secretary Xi Jinping made a solemn pledge that the Party would always stand with the people, be heedful of their aspirations, be accountable to them, and work hard for the common good.

Since then, the central leadership of the CPC has, with courage and determination, guided the nation through an extremely difficult stage of the reform process, in the face of complex challenges both at home and abroad. Thanks to innovative policies, we have been able to resolve many long-standing and thorny issues that previously defied solution and accomplished many tasks that could not be achieved in the past. These achievements have already drawn worldwide attention. The promise made five years ago has been fulfilled.

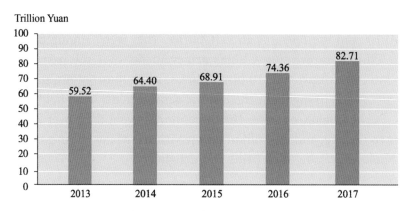

GDP Growth 2013-2017

These were five years of dramatic growth in our economy and in the comprehensive strength of the nation as a whole. GDP has increased from 54 trillion yuan to over 80 trillion yuan, second in the world, with an average annual growth rate of 7.1 percent, making China one of the world's fastest growing major economies. China's contribution to global economic growth has stayed above 30 percent, providing both an engine and stabilizing factor for the world economy. China has the world's largest expressway and high-speed railroad networks; innovations are happening and new technologies are being developed; major infrastructure projects are being built across the country. The modern time "Four Inventions", namely high-speed rail, mobile payment services, bike-share, and online shopping, have deeply transformed the Chinese society.

These were five years of great benefit to the people. Per capita disposable income increased to 23,821 yuan in 2016 from 16,510 yuan in 2012, an average annual growth of 7.4 percent, higher than the GDP growth rate. Engel's coefficient for households – the proportion of income allocated for food purchases – was 30.1 percent in 2016, close to what the UN regards as

High-speed Rail

Bike Share

Mobile Payment

Online Shopping

a relatively high living standard. With an increasing number of new social welfare programs, people are more secure, satisfied and happier. An extensive old-age pension system was put in place covering 900 million people; 1.35 billion people have basic health insurance; over 60 million people have been lifted out of poverty, which lowered the poverty rate from 10.2 percent to less than 4 percent. It was a miracle for China, and it is also an achievement that greatly contributes to global poverty reduction.

These were also five years of major progress in strengthening democracy and the rule of law. Democratic socialist institution building with Chinese characteristics has been ongoing, ensuring the primary role of the people. In 2013, the National People's Congress used a new representation formula for the first time for the election of delegates to its 12th NPC session, whereby members were elected based on the equal number of electorates in both rural and urban areas. This increased the number of worker and farmer representatives by 5.1 percent. Institutional reform has made substantive headway, with new measures aimed at streamlining government and delegating authority, cutting back red tape, and thus improving service and efficiency. A total of 618 items were declared exempt from review and approval by departments under the State Council. National oversight mechanisms are being overhauled to ensure that public officials are always subject to oversight in their exercise of authority. The rule of law has been strengthened as we continue to refine our socialist legal system with Chinese characteristics. With major headway made in the reform of the judicial system, there is now a higher level of legal awareness among CPC and government officials, and among the public at large. The concept of the rule of law is now more deeply imbedded in our forms of governance, government policies and in all aspects of the society.

During this period we have become more confident in our culture. This is imperative if we are to mobilize our people to build a strong country and achieve national renewal. Adapting Marxism to a new Chinese context makes it more relevant to guiding us towards the future. Education on core socialist values is promoting ethical behavior, encouraging many role models and inspiring more to follow. The mainstream media continues to grow, accompanied by an extensive media convergence, and a growing and healthy cyberspace environment. China's cultural industries are also booming.

Artistic creation is reaching new heights, producing quality works that have both substance and feeling, and that give moral and ethical direction.

During this time, progress on the diplomatic front has also been remarkable. China proposed the idea of a global community of shared future, rolled out the Belt and Road Initiative, hosted the APEC Beijing Summit and the G20 Hangzhou Summit, launched the Silk Road Fund and the Asian Infrastructure Investment Bank, hosted the Conference on Interaction and Confidence-Building Measures in Asia (CICA) in Shanghai and the BRICS summit in Xiamen. With its diplomatic activities proceeding on multiple fronts and in all directions, China is playing an ever growing role on the world stage. We are also an active part of the efforts in the reform of global governance, and will take on more international responsibilities to contribute positively to world peace and development.

There is no doubt these five years of hard work have paid off richly. In the long history of a nation, five years could go by in a flash, but the many accomplishments have greatly boosted the Chinese people's pride and confidence, propelling social and economic progress, and accelerating China's march towards national renewal.

HISTORIC SIGNIFICANCE OF THE ACHIEVEMENTS AND CHANGES

Since the summer of 2017, a number of influential and stirring documentaries have been aired, including *The Reform Continues*, *Amazing China*, and *Our Founding Mission, Our Forward Journey*, capturing the imagination of millions. Each from a different perspective presents a panoramic picture of the impressive economic and social progress over the past five years, inspiring and encouraging the people to move ahead.

These past five years were a defining period in Chinese history. Seemingly "impossible" obstacles have been overcome. Changes have been unprecedented, wide-ranging and far-reaching. General Secretary Xi Jinping characterized their significance as all-encompassing, trailblazing, in-depth, and substantive.

First, all-encompassing. The Central Committee led by Xi Jinping pursued an integrated approach that included overall planning so that reforms could proceed steadily in economy, society and culture. Other areas included foreign policy, national defense, domestic governance, environmental protection, Party building, and the promotion of ethical values in society. Progress has been remarkable in all areas, and momentum created for further economic and social development.

Second, trailblazing. The Central Committee, with great courage and determination, crafted a series of new strategies and policies based on original ideas and innovative concepts. Corresponding measures and actions were launched, opening up new perspectives and injecting fresh dynamism into the reforms.

Third, in-depth. Over 1,500 reform measures were rolled out, covering all major areas and addressing some of the trickiest issues. The depth and breadth of the transformation is unprecedented in Chinese history, and in the world.

Fourth, substantive. The reforms have removed old restrictions and created new possibilities, thus bringing important changes to the CPC, the nation, the people, and the armed forces. Especially effective are the strict measures for Party building that include strong enforcement of Party discipline and high standards of probity. Such substantive changes within the CPC also affect all levels of government, and reverberate through society. They touch on fundamental issues and will have far-reaching ramifications.

Courage and perseverance have made it possible to beat heavy odds. The combination of both tangible and more subtle transformations have brought about historic changes to both the CPC and the country. We are gratified to be living at this momentous time, and to witness the significant events that are transforming our nation.

A NEW STARTING POINT

An uphill path is the hardest to climb, and the last stretch to the summit is the hardest of all. An old saying also warns us that there is always another

The Asian Infrastructure Investment Bank

The Asian Infrastructure Investment Bank (AIIB) opened for business in January 2016, and has become an important player in international capital markets. Members have increased to 84. More and more countries welcome it as a useful addition to the existing lineup of multilateral financial institutions, and as a contributor to healthy development of the world economy. Pictured here: AIIB headquarters.

mountain to ascend. This is a favorite expression of General Secretary Xi Jinping, reminding us not to bask in past glories but to anticipate difficulties ahead, which will demand greater daring, determination and wisdom.

The 19th CPC National Congress offered a thorough assessment of the challenges in our path, identifying the major stumbling blocks and hazards. CPC members are duty-bound to tackle them head-on and promote socialism with Chinese characteristics in the new era.

We must face problems without flinching. They may hinder our progress, but they are nothing to be afraid of. The most important thing is to look into the cause of the problems, and then develop effective solutions.

Proper and systematic analysis is indispensable. The problems before us are extremely complex, interconnected, and likely to set off chain reactions. It is important to employ dialectical and scientific methods to analyze issues on a case-by-case basis to identify their nature. Some have emerged as unavoidable outcomes of the development process at a certain stage; others are caused by man and could have been avoided; some must be dealt with without delay, while others must await the right conditions. We must have a clear picture of the issues before we can identify their priorities and develop considered and targeted solutions.

After analysis comes action. We must take up the responsibility and address the most urgent issues that affect development, hinder reform and preoccupy our people most. Timetables must be set, tasks and responsibilities clearly defined. In particular, we need sustained and concerted efforts in three major areas: risk prevention and crisis management, targeted poverty elimination, and pollution control and prevention.

RISK AWARENESS AND PREVENTION

As we know, a bucket's capacity is as big as its shortest board and that it can hold no water if there is a hole at the bottom. It is therefore essential to strengthen the weakest links and in particular reinforce the base. The same is true of Party building and national development. We must be on constant guard against risks, especially systemic ones, or else our progress towards national renewal may hit snags or even be derailed.

There are harsh lessons from history. Since the 19th century, attempts at national renewal have suffered repeated setbacks including invasions by Western powers, years of strife between warlords, brutal Japanese imperialist aggression, corrupt rule by KMT reactionaries, blockades imposed by Western countries, the rupture of Sino-Soviet ties, and ten years of turmoil during the "Cultural Revolution." All brought our nation to the edge of collapse.

Being prepared and vigilant. We anticipate the voyage ahead will be far from smooth sailing. Accomplishments are no cause for complacency; rather, they should remind us to remain prudent and on guard, so as not to make strategic or disruptive mistakes. Though our historic achievements and many transformations have ushered in a new era of socialism with Chinese characteristics, the path to national renewal will be uneven, and hard work lies ahead.

Standing now at a new starting point, we have an opportunity to make history. The overall outlook is promising, but there are many risks both external and internal, major and minor. The international environment is unpredictable, our relations with neighboring countries complex and sensitive, and we must sustain a steady process of reform. Such circumstances demand a mentality of risk awareness and being prepared for all eventualities. Preventive measures must go hand in hand with risk management and resolution strategies. While forestalling risks comes first, we must have effective mechanisms in place to defuse them and turn them into opportunities. In short, we must always be prepared to overcome difficulties as we face up to new challenges on our forward march.

We can look back with pride at past accomplishments, and look forward to brighter prospects. We are in for a great new era to build a prosperous and beautiful China.

Q & A

Question: What is being done to "streamline administration"?

Answer: The government has been working to improve governance and efficiency so that it can provide better support to China's socialist market economy. These efforts include streamlining government functions and delegating authority, cutting red tape and rationalizing regulations, and providing better services. Specifically, we will reduce the number of items that require government approval, enforce effective regulations in different forms, and offer more and better services, to create a vibrant, fair and effective market environment that encourages innovation.

Historic significance of changes since the 18th CPC National Congress

Lin Zhaomu (Research Fellow at the Academy of Macroeconomic Research, National Development and Reform Commission): The changes since the 18th CPC National Congress are unparalleled in the history of the CPC and nation. They have been groundbreaking, extensive, and highly effective, laying the groundwork for our long-term progress. They are key to realizing the two Centennial Goals and fulfilling the dream of national renewal.

DEFINING THE THEORETICAL FRAMEWORK

—Understanding Xi Jinping Thought on Socialism with Chinese Characteristics for a New Era

At the beginning of November 2017, Volume II of *Xi Jinping: The Governance of China* was released, with an English version for international audiences. It has become a bestseller in China, and also sparked widespread interest abroad. It is Xi Jinping's second book on the governance of China, which offers further authoritative insights into what he means by socialism with Chinese characteristics in a new era, and explains its essential ideas and principles.

New guidelines are needed for a new era. One of the important contributions of the 19th CPC National Congress was the decision to affirm Xi Jinping Thought on Socialism with Chinese Characteristics for a New Era as part of the CPC's guiding philosophy, and to incorporate it into the Constitution of the CPC. This move ensures that the CPC's thinking evolves with the times in line with the wishes of the people and the Party, and that we will have purpose and direction for the future.

NEW REALITIES CALL FOR NEW THINKING

Just as a river flows from its source, Xi Jinping Thought on Socialism with Chinese Characteristics for a New Era has evolved within the wider context of socialism with Chinese characteristics. It has grown out of a new era of changing international relations, a new stage of further domestic reforms, and a self-revolution within the CPC that requires great courage.

New realities require new solutions. A dramatically changing world provides both opportunities and challenges. The wide-ranging and far-reaching transformations on our home front are moving China closer to the international center stage. It is important to have a clear focus in a complicated environment, and to grasp important opportunities to maintain a strategic initiative.

Xi Jinping: The Governance of China (volumes I and II) is a collection of his speeches, conversations and written comments during the period from the conclusion of the Party's 18th National Congress (2012) up to September 29, 2017. They provide an authoritative insight into Xi Jinping Thought on Socialism with Chinese Characteristics for a New Era.

New economic imperatives call for fresh guidance. Sustained reform efforts over the decades have created the China miracle, but we are also plagued with growing pains. The days of serious shortages of food and supplies are behind us, but imbalances and inadequacies in our development have come to the fore. While products "Made in China" are sold around the world, those "Created in China" are only just appearing. The material and cultural conditions of the people have substantially improved, but they hope for more. We urgently need guidance to deal with these new challenges, to improve the quality and efficiency of products and services, maintain robust growth, and succeed in building a moderately prosperous society in this new era.

The CPC also needs new direction. As the world's largest political party governing the world's largest developing country, it is facing both opportunities and challenges. Party building on the whole is going smoothly, but a number of problems remain. Guidance is thus needed for CPC members to enhance their political awareness, keep to the larger goals of the Party, follow the Party central leadership, and align their work with the agenda of the Party. The CPC must also be able to cleanse, improve, and reform itself, to encourage cohesion and effectiveness.

It was under such an overall background of the times that new thinking emerged, as represented by Xi Jinping Thought on Socialism with Chinese Characteristics for a New Era. This is a bold and serious attempt to combine theory with practice to systematically answer a number of basic questions in the new context: what kind of socialism should we pursue, and how can we do it? His thinking draws on the experience of both the CPC and people, and is a distillation of their collective wisdom. It adapts Marxism to a new Chinese context, and constitutes an important addition to the general theoretical framework of socialism with Chinese characteristics. It will provide guidance for the CPC and the people in their efforts to bring about national renewal.

Theory is born of practice and Xi Jinping Thought on Socialism with Chinese Characteristics for a New Era has evolved to deal with new imperatives. Since the 18th CPC National Congress, socialism with Chinese characteristics has continued to extend to cover overall economic, political, cultural, and social development, and environmental protection. It also includes a four-pronged strategy that calls for completing the building of a moderately prosperous society, executing all-round and in-depth reforms, promoting the rule of law and enforcing strict Party discipline. For the economy, there is the need to adjust to the new normal, boost supply-side structural reforms, and address rural issues involving farming and farmers, in a drive to upgrade and modernize the economy. In the area of poverty alleviation, the experience of past efforts has led to enhanced programs of targeted poverty reduction. On the diplomatic front, we have been pursuing an innovative and distinctly Chinese foreign policy that includes promoting international cooperation through the Belt and Road Initiative, and our proposal to build a global community of shared future. For Party building, we have taken actions to strengthen internal oversight and enforce stricter discipline in an effort to make the CPC a strong political party. It is fair to say that without all the practice and transformations of the last five years, there would have been no grounds for any new theory.

Given General Secretary Xi Jinping's important contributions and essential role in developing this new thinking, it is only appropriate that it was named after him. This decision reflects CPC's maturity and confidence as it enriches its theories.

A COMPREHENSIVE THEORETICAL FRAMEWORK

Clear reasoning and substance impart insight and power to a theory. Xi Jinping Thought on Socialism with Chinese Characteristics for a New Era is original and uniquely suited to China. It is a comprehensive and well-desgined theoretical framework that covers economy, politics, culture, social development, environment, as well as reforms, foreign policy, national defense and Party building.

To understand it, it is necessary to look at its basic premise and each component, and understand the ideas and concepts behind them, how they are related and why. With this understanding, we will be able to better apply the theory with its rich and comprehensive content.

The basic premise of this theory is how to build socialism with Chinese characteristics. This underscores all the different stages of China's development. After the 18th CPC National Congress, we started a new chapter in a new era of socialism with Chinese characteristics, and this basic premise continues to tie together all components of CPC's guiding philosophy and its governance practices. It is an important premise by which to understand the essence of the theory.

The core of Xi Jinping Thought on Socialism with Chinese Characteristics for a New Era is built on Eight Focus Areas. Each is important in itself, and each has a general goal, an overall plan and major issues to tackle. Together they present our approach to promoting economic, political, cultural, and social development, and environmental protection. They also include the four-pronged strategy of building a moderately prosperous society, furthering reform, improving the rule of law, and strengthening Party discipline, along with foreign policy and national defense. The Eight Focus Areas give us an overall picture of what is needed to achieve our goals and effectively perform our tasks.

The value of a sound theory is that it not only throws light on "what" but also provides direction as to "how." The "Fourteen Commitments" highlighted in the report to the 19th CPC National Congress are just such general directions for "what to do", and they represent an application of Xi Jinping Thought on Socialism with Chinese Characteristics for a New Era. Each targets a specific area and will serve as guidelines for turning theory into action.

The Eight Focus Areas and Fourteen Commitments are major components of Xi Jinping Thought on Socialism with Chinese Characteristics for a New Era. They are mutually reinforcing, and must be implemented in a coordinated way. The Eight Focus Areas represent the guiding philosophy on what kind of socialism to pursue and develop in the new era. The Fourteen Commitments are action-oriented, about what to do to achieve the goal. Together they are a combination of theory and practice, and of strategy and tactics, as a key feature of the theory. They provide guidance on both theoretical and practical levels, and help identify trends and patterns in complex issues so that we can respond with confidence and skill.

The theory has both breadth and depth, and requires careful study to fully understand its significance, and appreciate the truth and wisdom it contains.

WHY IS THE THEORY SIGNIFICANT?

In early 2017, a series of short videos went viral on social media. In these videos, an international student from Peking University interviewed fellow foreign residents about their life in China, especially about what they really liked most and the response included the omnipresent smartphones, easy and simple mobile payment, convenient bike-sharing, and the amazing high-speed rail network. Indeed, the Chinese society is changing in mind-boggling ways.

So what has made this possible? As we look at the great changes taking place in cities and rural areas, in coastal regions and inland areas, from north of the Great Wall to south of the Yangtze River, it is clear that they are the result of applying Xi Jinping Thought on Socialism with Chinese Characteristics for a New Era.

Politically speaking, it offers a new direction. People must be rallied to the same cause before concerted actions can happen. To build political unity and cohesion in a huge country like ours with such a large governing party, the key is a guiding theory that both empowers and inspires. Xi Jinping Thought on Socialism with Chinese Characteristics for a New Era is creative, clarifying, and provides a political vision of shared goals that can rally the Party and the people. Practice has already and will continue to demonstrate that it is the only guiding theory capable of resolving the many problems ahead.

Historically speaking, it is significant because thanks to it, we are closer than we have ever been to national renewal, a goal for which generations of Chinese have fought and sacrificed over the last century. Xi Jinping Thought on Socialism with Chinese Characteristics for a New Era answers the question "where we came from, where we are going." It describes the deeper meaning of national renewal, lays out the ways to achieve it, and provides the intellectual power and direction for us to advance towards our goal.

On a theoretical level, it adds new dimensions to Marxism. Our commitment to basic Marxist principles remains unchanged, but a new context requires new thinking. Adapting Marxism to current realities is CPC's fundamental position. Xi Jinping Thought on Socialism with Chinese Characteristics for a New Era, rooted in classical Marxist philosophy and the basic principles of scientific socialism, is in step with the modern times. With its new thinking and strategies, it represents the Chinee version of Marxism, in another big step forward in applying Marxist principles to the Chinese context. Marxism has been enriched for the 21st century and continues to enjoy its relevance in today's China.

Practically speaking, it has guided China's development from one success to another. Forward-looking ideas are key to delivering tangible results, and thanks to them, China has experienced profound changes in all aspects of life, boosting the Chinese people's pride and confidence as never before.

It also has an international component. Today the world is at a crossroads. Which way should it head? Xi Jinping Thought on Socialism with Chinese Characteristics for a New Era, after careful analysis, proposes an alternative path for those nations wishing to accelerate their development while protecting their independence from outside interference. This is a contribution to the collective wisdom of mankind.

Theories evolve with the times. A new era brings new issues, which give rise to new thinking, which in turn guides action. China is an old civilization; it is also a young republic, emerging from the past and marching into a new era. Under the guidance of Xi Jinping Thought on Socialism with Chinese Characteristics for a New Era, we will add new chapters to the saga of national renewal.

The Eight Areas of Focus

These are as follows:

Pursuing socialism with Chinese characteristics to realize socialist modernization and national renewal. After building a moderately prosperous society, a two-step approach will be taken to build China, by the middle of the century, into a great, modern, socialist country that is prosperous, strong, democratic, culturally advanced, harmonious, and beautiful.

Resolving imbalanced and inadequate development to satisfy people's growing desire for a better life. This is the major challenge in the new era. We are committed to a people-centered development philosophy, and will promote human development so as to achieve prosperity for all.

Promoting economic, political, cultural, and social development, and environmental protection as our general approach, operationalized through a four-pronged strategy of building a moderately prosperous society, implementing a wider in-depth reform agenda, strengthening the rule of law, and tightening Party discipline. We must have confidence in our path, our guiding theory, our political system, and our values.

Advancing China's national governance system and capacity through further reforms.

Strengthening the legal system with Chinese characteristics and building a socialist country based on the rule of law.

Fulfilling the Party's goal for national defense, to build a disciplined, world-class and effective military under CPC's command.

Fostering a new model of international relations and building a global community of shared future as part of our major country diplomacy.

Recognizing that leadership by the CPC is the defining feature of socialism with Chinese characteristics. The CPC represents the highest level of political power, hence the importance of Party building.

The Fourteen Commitments

We remain committed to:
leadership by the CPC in all aspects;
a people-centered approach;
further reform;
a new vision for development;
the will of the people;
the rule of law;
core socialist values;
popular well-being;
harmony between man and nature;
national security in all respects;
CPC's total control over the armed forces;
the principle of "one country, two systems" and national reunification;
a global community of shared future; and strict Party discipline.

CHAPTER 5

LEADING THE WAY FORWARD

—Understanding the historical mission of the CPC in the new era

One week after the closing of the 19th CPC National Congress in October 2017, General Secretary Xi Jinping took the newly elected Standing Committee of the Politburo of the CPC Central Committee on a special trip to the places where the CPC started almost a century ago. They renewed their oath at the site of the 1st CPC National Congress in Shanghai, and then went to Jiaxing County, Zhejiang Province, where they recalled the mission of the CPC in front of a red boat on the South Lake, the second site of the same congress. As they followed the footsteps of early Communists and revisited the birthplace of the CPC, the central leadership of the CPC demonstrated a strong sense of mission and responsibility to continue their journey for national renewal, with the support and approval of the people.

Never forget where you started, and your mission can be completed. Ninety-seven years ago, the Communist Party of China took upon itself a great historical mission for national renewal and generations of Chinese Communists, with enormous devotion and commitment, have since fought in unceasing battles to achieve its goals. The CPC Central Committee's report to its 19th National Congress recalled the hardships and difficulties that the CPC had gone through to complete its historic mission and called on the whole party to work together to continue its cause in the new era.

LOFTY IDEAL AND ULTIMATE GOAL

On June 29th, 1921, Xie Juezai, a veteran revolutionary at the time, made this entry in his diary: "At 6 pm, Shuheng[1] left for Shanghai, together with Runzhi[2], for the "National". To make sure that his words did not cause any

---

1 Shuheng, referring to He Shuheng, was one of the 13 delegates for the 1st CPC National Congress.
2 Runzhi was the courtesy name of the late Chairman Mao Zedong, who was also a delegate to the 1st CPC National Congress.

The site of the first CPC National Congress in 1921

suspicion to the authorities, he used five circles to refer to "communists". The "National Congress of the Communists", held in a nondescript building in Shanghai, was to become a cause that rallied countless people to join the CPC with their dedication and determination to fight for the goal of communism.

Communism represents mankind's highest ideal for a society, and it embodies people's urge and aspirations for a better future. It is a scientific thought, like a rising sun that lights up the road for humanity to advance towards an ideal society. Communism is also a real and concrete movement that has profoundly changed the course of world history, and the lives of hundreds of millions of people. Upon its establishment, the CPC took communism as its ideal and ultimate goal, with a mission to improve the lot of the Chinese people and make the Chinese nation strong again. In its 97 years of history, the CPC has always kept in mind the aspiration and future of the nation and the wellbeing of the Chinese people as it forged on towards the ultimate goal of communism.

Communism is the unshakable belief of the Chinese Communists. It is an ideal and conviction that the CPC has kept alive all the time. The CPC is called the Communist Party because it is a party that has been engaged in a sustained pursuit of communism. For nearly a century, communism, as CPC's profound conviction, has inspired generations of Communists, and thousands of people have given their lives for the ideal. "I may lose my life, but I'll never lose my conviction." It was a vow that testified to CPC members' commitment to the lofty ideal of communism. This firm belief has kept the CPC strong, going through untold hardships and sacrifices to become what it is today.

Communism is like a beacon, guiding the nation on its way to rejuvenation. As the ultimate form of human society, communism represents the inevitable trend of social development and a historical process in which the society advances to its highest form. The ultimate goal of the CPC, communism is also an ideal that guides the Chinese nation in its efforts to achieve national renewal. With a bright future in mind, we know where we want to go, and with the goals set, we know where our efforts should be placed. Communism is a great banner that rallies the Chinese people to make the nation prosperous and strong.

Communism is like a vision, a beautiful prospect that inspires people forward, a prospect where people have their faith, the country is strong, and the nation has a bright future. In the ideal society of communism, there is a high level of productivity, abundant supply and freedom of personal development. Exploitation is completely eliminated, and there is no more rich or poor. As the *Communist Manifesto* says, communism is an independent movement participated by the vast majority of people and for the benefit of the majority. This is a great undertaking that will inspire generation after generation of the Chinese people in their efforts to create a better life for everyone.

Communism cannot be realized overnight. It is a lofty goal to be achieved in stages, and it is a process of continuous advancement. As we pursue socialism with Chinese characteristics, we are actually applying the principles of communism in practice, in a way that will bring us closer to achieving our ultimate goal. First, however, we need to work on our immediate tasks, to promote socialism with Chinese characteristics and achieve national renewal.

The ideal of communism, however, should be kept alive at all times, not to be forgotten or lost because of the extraordinary amount of time needed for its realization. For these reasons, we must continue our efforts to advance socialism with Chinese characteristics, with full confidence in our chosen path, political system, guiding theories and values, towards achieving the ultimate goal.

A HISTORIC MISSION FOR NATIONAL RENEWAL

The Chinese nation is a great nation with a history of more than 5,000 years. It has created a magnificent civilization that has made indelible contributions to the progress of human civilization as a whole. Starting from the Opium War in the mid-19th century, however, the Chinese nation was plunged into years of darkness with wars, foreign invasions, struggling economy, social instability and widespread poverty. There were numerous attempts in these years to save the country and revive the nation, but none succeeded.

In 1921, the Communist Party of China was established, an epoch-making event in the history of China that opened a new chapter in the Chinese revolution. The CPC became a party that the Chinese people looked to for national independence, liberation, national prosperity and a better life. For the first time in history, the Chinese people could really have their will represented, as countless Chinese Communists took up the fight for the people and for the rejuvenation of the nation.

During the war years, numerous Chinese Communists laid down their lives for national liberation. According to available statistics, more than 3.7 million people died from 1921 to 1949 fighting under the leadership of the CPC, and these were just deaths that could be accounted for. It was a sacrifice no other political party in the world had ever experienced. For 28 years the CPC had led the Chinese people in an arduous struggle through countless hardships and sacrifices to finally win the victory in the new democratic revolution, overthrowing imperialism, feudalism, and bureaucratic capitalism. The nation and the people won their independence and emancipation. The nation made a great leap forward from thousands of years of feudal and authoritarian rule to a country founded on the basis of people's democracy.

During the years of national reconstruction, the Chinese Communists again made a huge contribution, as represented by thousands of role models in different lines of work. Thanks to the dedication and hard work of the Chinese people under the leadership of the CPC, China had completed its socialist revolution and established the basic structure for a socialist system. It is the political and institutional foundation for any development and progress in contemporary China, and for China to advance from a weak nation to what it is today and continue to achieve its future goals.

During the years of reform and opening up, the Chinese Communists were the pioneers pushing for all-round reforms that brought about unprecedented development in both the rural and urban areas, from the coast to inland, with important progress in economy, politics, culture, society, environment, etc., in great strides to catch up with the times. Thanks to determined reforms and innovations under the leadership of the CPC, the Chinese people have removed the ideological and institutional obstacles that hinder development and have taken on the path of socialism with Chinese characteristics. This has brought historical changes to the country, to the life of the Chinese people, and to the Communist Party of China.

For almost a century, the Communist Party of China has fought endless battles and gone through untold hardships and sacrifices to fulfill its mission for the people and the nation, with the same dedication and determination, and has proven that it has lived up to the expectations of the people and it is a political party that is worthy of the times. It is the right choice to lead the great endeavor for national renewal. To set the right goals and continue on our path of success, however, we must take a look at where we came from, how far we have gone, where we plan to go next and learn from the experience of others.

CONTINUOUS EFFORTS FOR NATIONAL RENEWAL

In his famous article in 1930 "A Single Spark Can Start a Prairie Fire", the late Chairman Mao Zedong described the Chinese revolution as "a ship emerging on the horizon, or the morning sun that is rising in the east." Today, we are closer than ever before to achieving our goals, and we have the confidence and capability greater than ever before to fulfill our mission. It is a dream that is coming true, as we can now see the tip of the mast and the radiant glow of the rising sun. As we get closer to the goal, we must redouble our efforts, and also be aware that this is an endeavor that needs a huge amount of effort, stronger leadership by the CPC and full commitment by the people.

We know that we need to make greater efforts for national rejuvenation. It is a process of hard work and challenges. There are many obstacles ahead of us, and we must put up the same fight as we did in the war years to conquer them. We will lose out in our final battle if we become lax and complacent, not being able to take the issues head on. We must fully understand that this is a long and difficult process with emerging and complicated issues. We must therefore continue our efforts with the same dedication, and firm commitment to the leadership of the CPC and the interests of the people.

We know that we need the strong leadership by the CPC for national rejuvenation. For nearly a hundred years, the Communist Party of China has been the pioneer and backbone for the renewal of the Chinese nation. History has proved and will continue to prove that without CPC leadership, national renewal would be an elusive goal. But the CPC also faces enormous challenges in different areas as it leads the nation in the long and difficult process towards this goal. The CPC must therefore take on the important task of Party building, to make it a party with strong political leadership, clear theoretical guidance, and exceptional ability to mobilize and rally the people around its cause. This must be done before the CPC can garner further successes in the nation's drive for national renewal.

We know that we need the full commitment to socialism with Chinese characteristics. It is a system that has taken root in this land thanks to China's reform and opening up policies. It has created one miracle after another, injecting vitality into this ancient nation and bringing its people closer to the goal of national renewal. As we look back at the journey we have covered, we are confident that we have the path leading to a better life, the theoretical guidance that steers our way forward, the system that safeguards our progress, and the culture that bonds our people together. We have every reason to believe in and follow socialism with Chinese characteristics with its path, theoretical guidance, institutions, and culture. We will forge on without any fear and free of any interference, to make sure that the train for national rejuvenation advances on the right track heading for a bright tomorrow.

The grand Chinese dream requires greater efforts, a strong CPC leadership and total commitment from the people. With the dream, we have the course of action for our efforts. As we make greater efforts to achieve our goals, we are taking up the responsibility. The CPC leadership provides an important support to our efforts. And we have the people's full commitment to socialism with Chinese characteristics. The CPC leadership, as always, will be a decisive factor in all of our efforts. As we continue to pursue socialism with Chinese characteristics in the new era, we will need the efforts, CPC leadership and the full commitment of the people in order to achieve our dream for national renewal.

We must always remember where we came from, no matter how far we have gone. A nation that does not remember its past has no future and a political party that has forgotten its mission will not go far. The Communist Party of China started with only a few dozen members and is now a political party with a membership 89 million strong, just like a single small boat having turned into a giant ocean-going ship. The Communist Party of China, which will celebrate its centenary in a few years' time, is still in its prime time, and will keep to its mission and its original aspirations as it leads a united people towards a bright future.

CPC members must make more conscious efforts in the following five areas:

To uphold the leadership of the CPC and the socialist system, and oppose any words or actions that weaken, distort, and negate them;

To safeguard the interests of the people and oppose any action that may alienate the people and harm their interests;

To be part of the drive for reform and innovation in the new era and help solve long-standing issues and remove obstacles to progress.

To safeguard China's sovereignty, security, and development, and oppose any acts that attempt to split the nation and undermine national unity and social stability; and

To prevent and control various risks and overcome difficulties and challenges that may emerge in politics, economy, culture, society, and the natural environment.

CPC: the initiator, leader and practitioner for national renewal

Qu Qingshan (Director of the Office of CPC History under the CPC Central Committee)

The history of the CPC is one of unremitting efforts by its members to achieve national renewal. The CPC is the initiator, leader and practitioner of this great cause. It has been committed to its historic mission at all times, and has the courage to correct its errors and fight the battles against heavy odds. It has rallied the people to the great cause of national renewal and taken the nation from victory to victory.

CHAPTER 6

LAYING OUT AMBITIOUS PLANS

—Understanding the strategic plans for socialism with Chinese characteristics in the new era

On October 1, 1949, Chairman Mao Zedong solemnly proclaimed to the world the founding of the People's Republic of China. The Chinese people had stood up, and the Chinese nation's hundred-year journey towards building a modern country had begun. By the middle of the 21st century, China will have achieved the goal of modernization as it becomes a strong and advanced socialist country. This will be a magnificent achievement that the Chinese people have fought for with resolve and determination through a century of hard struggle.

Entering the new era, socialism with Chinese characteristics stands at a new starting point, having already completed the "first half" of the journey of modernization. At its 19th National Congress, the CPC mapped out strategic plans for the remaining 30 years to complete the second half of the journey to build a moderately prosperous society and make China a modern socialist nation.

A BLUEPRINT FOR THE NEW JOURNEY

Over 170 years ago, the Opium War of 1840 forced open the doors of an isolated imperial China, awakening the nation from the dream world of the "Heavenly Kingdom". Reformers searched hard for ways to modernize the nation, proposing many different ideas and strategies for national salvation, but all attempts failed in one way or another, whether it was the Westernization Movement in the late 19th century, the short lived Hundred-Day Reform in 1898, the efforts to enact a constitution at the beginning of the 20th century, or the 1911 Republican Revolution.

The birth of the Communist Party of China brought hope for national salvation. For 28 years since it was founded in 1921, the CPC led the Chinese people in a long struggle for independence and liberation, and at the cost of much blood and many sacrifices, succeeded in overthrowing imperialism, feudalism, and bureaucratic-capitalism, finally establishing the new republic in 1949, thus opening up the road towards full modernization.

This road can be compared to a relay race that will need the efforts of several generations to reach the final goal. At each critical juncture in the country's development, the CPC was able to respond to the changing times and propose strategies for the next phase of progress. Shortly after 1949, the CPC proposed the goal of modernizing industry, agriculture, national defense, and science and technology to transform China into a strong socialist country. With the launch of the reform and opening up policy in 1978, the CPC laid out strategic plans for the modernization process. In 1987, the CPC's 13th National Congress proposed a "three-stage" development strategy to lead the country out of a subsistence economy to a moderately prosperous society. This was a gigantic stride of historic significance. In 1997, at its 15th National Congress, the CPC again proposed a new "three-stage" strategy that laid out objectives to be completed by 2010, 2021 (the 100th anniversary of the founding of the CPC), and 2049, the centenary of the founding of the People's Republic. Thanks to nearly 70 years of efforts since the founding of the PRC, and especially the efforts of the last 40 years since the reforms began, the country is now in a more advanced stage of development, with the prospect of full modernization by the middle of the century.

The 19th CPC National Congress has gone one step further by laying out a specific roadmap for development over the next 30 years, to complete the building of a moderately prosperous society by 2020, and after that, to build a fully modernized socialist nation by the middle of the century. This Second Centennial Goal will be achieved in two stages: an initial 15 years until 2035 to achieve basic modernization, and then another 15 years until 2049 during which we will redouble our efforts to further build China into a strong, modern and prosperous socialist country with a sound democratic system, harmonious society, and beautiful environment. These objectives are a rallying call, galvanizing the nation and the people to advance towards them.

A MODERATELY PROSPEROUS SOCIETY

A better life has been the dream of the Chinese people for thousands of years. Since it was founded, a primary goal of the CPC has always been to better the lot of the common man, and now it has pledged to both the people and history to complete by 2020 the process of building a moderately prosperous society. Achieving this will be an important milestone on the journey towards national rejuvenation. We are only three years away and victory is in sight, We are excited that the First Centennial Goal will soon become a reality.

We have therefore arrived at the moment for the final push. Specific tasks and objectives for these last three years were laid out at the 19th CPC National Congress. Time is short, so tasks and challenges must be tackled with the greatest urgency and initiative to win final victory. An integrated approach is essential to meet challenges in a changed context, with special focus on weak areas. For continued healthy growth, particular efforts are needed in the following three areas: risk prevention and control, targeted poverty reduction, and pollution prevention.

Risk prevention and control. We often say, "When safe, remember danger; with success, remember failure; with order, remember chaos." From now until 2020, risks and dangers may build up and manifest themselves at the same time. A greater sense of prevention and a better ability to manage them are essential to handling them effectively. We cannot allow external risks to become internal ones, or economic and financial risks to evolve into political and social ones, or discrete risks to turn into systemic ones. Throughout this period, there must be heightened awareness of and consistent efforts to prevent and control risks.

Targeted poverty reduction. As of the end of 2017, there were still 30 million people nationwide living in poverty, many in remote areas in extreme destitution. They are the primary targets for poverty alleviation efforts. The overall number of impoverished people has dropped considerably, but the task of reducing it further has become more challenging. Many sectors must be mobilized and measures taken to focus on removing constraining factors and inadequacies. Large poverty alleviation programs must be implemented with targeted plans for poor villages and individual families. At the same time, better social guarantees and tilted policies must be put in place to make sure that no one is left behind on the journey towards a moderately prosperous society.

Pollution prevention and control. China today continues to face serious environmental challenges. The living environment is still not as good as people desire. Green development must be promoted with an emphasis on conservation, protection, and natural recovery. This will require increased efforts to transform and upgrade industries and optimize land resource use. Prominent environmental issues that undermine public health and are of highest concern to people must be addressed so we can create a peaceful, harmonious and beautiful homeland.

WHAT IS BASICALLY ACHIEVING THE GOAL OF MODERNIZATION?

At its 13th National Congress in 1987, the CPC proposed that China basically achieve the goal of socialist modernization by the middle of the 21st century. The recent 19th CPC National Congress, however, moved the goal forward by 15 years to 2035. Such a major strategic decision was made based on an assessment of China's present development and its future trend. It demonstrates the strength of socialism with Chinese characteristics in the new era, moving forward in great confidence.

So what is meant by basically achieving the goal of socialist modernization? In a nutshell, it means basic modernization in five areas: economy, politics, culture, the society and ecology and environment.

A modern economic system will be in place. By 2035, China will have taken a major leap forward in its economy, science and technology. The economy will grow on an optimized structure, with its growth rate maintained at medium to high speed and its industries moving up to medium to high-end production. The economy will grow on improved quality and efficiency, not just size and scale. There will be greater economic vigor, more advanced world-class manufacturing industries, and a marked improvement in total-factor productivity. China will be an innovation driven economy by 2020, and will become one of the leading countries in innovation by 2035.

A modern, effective system of national governance will be in place. The people's right to participation and development will be fully guaranteed. As the foundation of the country, government and society, the rule of law will be strengthened. It is a country led by the CPC with a system that is based on the rule of law and people's full participation in the decision-making process through a refined people's congress system and the consultative democratic process. The rule of law will apply to all areas, and there will be more sound legislation, fair judicial practices, strict enforcement and widespread popular adherence .

Society will reach a higher level of civility. The country's cultural soft power will have grown, as the result of greater cultural confidence, awareness, and cohesion. The Chinese dream and the core values of socialism will have taken root; patriotism, collectivism, and socialism will be embraced by the people. Cultural services and sectors, and a market for cultural products will have been established. People will observe higher moral and ethical standards; they will be better educated, and healthier. China will have cultural exchanges with other countries in many more areas, and Chinese culture will be better known abroad.

Solid progress will have been made towards common prosperity. China will figure in the ranks of high-income countries, with a more comfortable life for its people and modern, effective social institutions. Everyone will have access to public services: child care, education, employment, medical care, elder care, shelter, social support, etc. Life expectancy and educational level will be among the tops in the world. The country will be run under a system where the government, the society and citizens will all play their proper role. People will feel better served, more satisfied and secure in a society that is sustainable, vibrant, orderly and harmonious.

The goal of a beautiful China will have been basically achieved. There will be a stronger set of measures supporting ecological protection, leading to a fundamentally improved environment. An efficient, safe, clean, and low-carbon energy structure will be in place, as well as a circular economy based on green, low-carbon development. Green development and a low-carbon life style will be the order of the day. A network of national ecological buffer zones will be in place. There will be substantial improvements of the air, water and soil quality. After peaking around 2030, China's total carbon emissions will decline, in itself an important contribution to global efforts to address climate change and promote green development.

A STRONG AND MODERN SOCIALIST COUNTRY

In 1954, the late Chairman Mao Zedong said, "We have full confidence in overcoming all difficulties and challenges to build our country into a great socialist republic. We are progressing, and we are doing glorious things that our predecessors have never done before." Today, more than six decades later, this great vision is coming true. When we reread his words, we are inspired and excited in our united resolve to achieve our final goal.

By the middle of the 21st century, we will have achieved our final goal to make China a strong, modern and prosperous socialist country, with considerable advancement in economy, politics, culture, society and environment.

What will China look like then?

China's national strength will be at an all-time high. There will be a substantial rise in productivity, placing the country among the world leaders in terms of core competitiveness. China will have an economy and market larger than any other country, giving it a leading position in comprehensive national strength and international influence. Our people will be more cultivated and educated, and the Chinese spirit, Chinese values, and Chinese strength will be driving the country in further development.

A more mature and structured system of governance will be in place. Up-to-date and effective governance provides the institutional basis for a strong socialist country. Over the next 30 years, one of the goals of China's reform agenda is to strengthen institution building by eliminating inadquacies and thus to put in place a more mature, comprehensive and formed system of governance. By fusing the rule of law with ethical principles of governance, a dynamic political environment will be created in which decisions are taken on the basis of wide participation, rules are observed while allowing for individual freedom, and the collective will and personal preferences coexist.

A better life for the Chinese people. Urban and rural incomes will rise, life will become more comfortable and public services more encompassing. Citizens will share equally in the national prosperity in an orderly, vibrant, fair and just society. Blue skies, green earth and clear water will become the norm, creating new harmony between man and nature.

China will be one of the strongest countries in the world. We are an ancient civilization with a long history, but we will demonstrate unprecedented vitality and contribute more to world peace and development. The Chinese nation is committed to the shared future of mankind.

The plans are laid out, and we are on track to success. China is a vast country with 1.3 billion people, an area of 9.6 million square kilometers, and a 5,000-year-old civilization. The Chinese people therefore have both the confidence and resolve to succeed in building socialism with Chinese characteristics in the new era, and in making China a strong and modern country. We have every reason to believe that we will achieve this goal.

An important experience of governance

Yang Weimin (Deputy Director of the General Office of the Financial Leading Group of the CPC Central Committee): An important experience of CPC governance is the formulation of different strategies for different stages of development. Over the years, these have been implemented by successive Party Central Committees one after the other. At its recent 19th National Congress, the CPC put forward a "two-stage" strategy that has moved the goal of socialist modernization forward by fifteen years. The Second Centennial Goal is also described in greater detail, and there are important timelines and roadmaps for achieving the goal.

The "three-stage" strategy of the 13th CPC National Congress

In October 1987, the 13th CPC National Congress put forward a "three-stage" development strategy for China's economy. In the first stage, between 1981 and 1990, the goal was to double GNP to ensure basic subsistence for the population, which was pretty much achieved by the end of the 1980s. In the second stage, between 1991 and the end of the 20th century, GNP was to double again for living standards to reach a level of moderate prosperity. In the third stage to be reached by the middle of the 21st century, per capita GNP was to reach the level of a medium developed country, and thus basically achieving modernization.

The new "three-stage" strategy of the 15th CPC National Congress

In 1997, the 15th CPC National Congress put forward a new "three-stage" strategy for the 21st century. In the first ten years, GNP would double on the basis of the figure for 2000, creating a reasonably sound socialist market system and a moderately prosperous life for the people. During the second ten years up to 2021, the 100th anniversary of the founding of the CPC, the national economy would continue to grow, and institutions and systems would improve. By the mid-21st century, when the People's Republic of China celebrates its 100th anniversary, modernization would be basically achieved, creating a strong and prosperous socialist country with significant democratic and cultural progress.

An important milestone: a moderately prosperous society

Han Wenxiu (Vice Minister, Research Office of the State Council): The goal of a moderately prosperous society and the goal of modernization are closely linked both in sequence and content. The former is necessary for the latter. Successfully creating a moderately prosperous society as planned will mean we have passed an important milestone and are ready to move on to the third stage of modernization. This is a highly significant juncture in our development.

Three major challenges to building a moderately prosperous society

The Central Economic Work Conference held in December 2017 pointed out that over the next three years, three major challenges would need primary attention: prevent and manage major risks and dangers, targeted poverty reduction, and pollution control.

1. In major risk prevention and control, the focus will be on financial risks. As supply-side structural reforms continue, a well-functioning financial system must be further developed, to consistently support the real economy and discourage excessive leveraging in the real estate market. Risks in key areas must be mitigated by suppressing illegal financial activities as well as tightening supervision where regulation is insufficient.

2. In poverty reduction, there must be qualitative alleviation based on present criteria. These must neither be lowered nor raised too high. Alleviation efforts must concentrate on seriously impoverished areas, target specific poor families, and motivate those affected to help themselves. Proper assessment and supervision are also necessary.

3. In pollution control, the priority is to reduce total discharges of major pollutants and to improve overall quality of the ecology and environment. A primary task is cutting air pollution, which requires industrial transformation by eliminating obsolete and excessive production capacity, adjusting energy and transportation structures, and increasing energy conservation and audits.

CHAPTER 7

ADVANCING TO THE NEXT STAGE

—Building a modern economy

Over 100 million in 11 seconds, 1 billion in 28 seconds, 10 billion in 3.1 minutes, and over 100 billion in 9 hours and 4 seconds.... Such was the turnover on Tmall during the "Double 11" (November 11th) online shopping bonanza, and it continued to reach new heights, eventually topping out at 168.2 billion RMB, breaking all previous records. During the event, over 100 million customers from 225 countries and regions participated via the Tmall shopping platform alone. It is fair to say that "Double 11" has become not only the most popular shopping event in China, but also one of the biggest shopping holidays in the world.

The online sales extravaganza of "Double 11" left the world in awe and demonstrated the immense vitality and infinite potential of the Chinese economy. On the basis of a careful assessment of China's economic fundamentals, a new vision for development and a strategy for building a modern economy were outlined at the 19th CPC National Congress, setting the direction for sustained and healthy economic development. They respond to the new realities in this new era of socialism with Chinese characteristics as well as the need for economic transformation and upgrading.

REORIENTING ECONOMIC GROWTH TOWARDS QUALITY

"China won." That was the title of the cover story of the Asian edition of the US periodical *Time* magazine released on November 13, 2017. The story presents one perspective of China's ever-growing impact on the rest of the world.

Regardless of what foreign critics may say, China has undoubtedly created a head-turning economic miracle in the 40 years since reform and opening up began. It has emerged as a major driver and stabilizer of global economic growth. However, as aggregate economic output continues to grow, we are confronted with new situations and issues. Currently, China's economy is at an important juncture as it goes through a change of growth model, structural optimization and a shift in growth drivers in a transition from high-speed growth to one of quality. Building a modern economic system would allow China to complete such a transition and lay a solid foundation for building a modern socialist country.

So, what exactly is a modern economic system? What should be the focus of any effort to build it? A modern economic system means prioritizing quality and results, promoting economic change, improving efficiency, changing growth drivers, improving total factor productivity, and enhancing innovation and competitiveness. More specifically, this means further supply-side structural reforms, innovation, a rural revitalization strategy and a regionally coordinated development strategy, a strong socialist market economy, and greater openness. In other words, a focus on supply-side reforms, building a more efficient industrial structure, and a stronger economic system.

Supply-side reform. Building a modern economy involves many aspects, so it is vital to focus on the crucial one that affects and drives all the others. Supply-side reform has already produced results, but at this point, there are still structural and systemic weakness that are the greatest limiting factors in the economy. More reforms are necessary. Our economic development must focus on building up the real economy and improving product quality to increase competitiveness, as well as creating a dynamic adjustment and balance between supply and demand.

A more efficient industrial structure means building a strong real economy driven by scientific and technological innovation and supported by modern financial services and human resources. The real economy is the primary component of China's economic development and the foundation of its industries. Building an efficient industrial structure with parallel progress in different sectors is the most dynamic and important contributor to China's economic development. It will channel more technology, capital and human resources into the real economy for efficient and quality production.

A robust economic system should enhance the effectiveness of market mechanisms, boost business dynamism, and ensure appropriate macro control. The success of China's market-oriented economic reforms would depend on a proper definition of the roles of the government and the market and how the "visible and invisible hands" function. The goal is to improve the socialist market economy so that the market can play a decisive role in resource allocation, while the government can better fulfill its own clearly-defined responsibilities. This should help break down barriers to business initiative, and build the systems and mechanisms to unleash innovation potential and strengthen competitiveness.

SUPPLY-SIDE STRUCTURAL REFORM

Beijing Oriental Electronics (BOE) was a company virtually unknown in the global LCD market about a decade ago, but a "dark horse" emerged and it has become a leader and a giant in the industry, after ten years of sustained efforts. Today, one out of every four tablet computers on the global market bears the brand BOE. One out of every five smartphones uses a BOE screen.

The successful emergence of BOE is a classic example of how supply-side structural reforms can bring real results. In recent years such reforms have

Super large LCD made by BOE

Slashing overcapacity: a success story in Bazhou City

In recent years, the city of Bazhou in Hebei Province has upgraded its industries and cut overcapacity to make a successful transition from a focus on quantity to quality. This is the result of combining industry with market mechanisms, government facilitation and supporting policies. Full acquisition by strategic investors allowed enterprises to upgrade, which promoted overall industry upgrading, and in turn led to regional upgrading. The photo shows a worker inspecting stored equipment.

dominated China's economic landscape. Specific actions have included capacity reduction, destocking, deleveraging, cost reduction, and fixing weaknesses, commonly referred to as "five priority measures". Other actions have involved comprehensive rural reform, reinvigorating the real economy, and stabilizing the real estate market. Significant progress has been made, and key industries and sectors have changed profoundly. New growth drivers are emerging; supply and demand are in better balance; improvement in quality and efficiency continues.

Popular wisdom tells us that only those who are willing to take on the hard tasks will be successful. Supply-side structural reform is extremely complex, involving a wide range of issues with far-reaching ramifications, including alignment of policies, laws, and mechanisms, as well as a fundamental shift in ways of thinking. More challenging tasks lie ahead. The supply-side reform guidelines outlined at the 19th CPC National Congress must be implemented, with a focus on strengthening the real economy, especially the manufacturing sector, and on improving the system of supply and demand. "The five priority measures" are critical for achieving a sound and dynamic supply-demand balance, thereby increasing China's economic advantages.

A larger range of quality products and services. Over the last few years, many new products and services have emerged. Here are some examples: bike-sharing that requires only a scan of a QR code, home delivery for online shopping, smart technology in the home, and others. We must always position ourselves at the forefront of global economic development trends and respond to new imperatives. These include encouraging creativity and innovation, pursuing green and low-carbon growth, developing the sharing economy, building modern supply chains, and providing more human services. As new models and forms of business appear, more individualized consumption needs can be met at all levels, both high-end and middle, producing new drivers for growth.

It is time to move up the value chain. Although China is a major manufacturing country and its products are sold around the world, it has long been stuck in the mid-to-low position within the global value chain, where the added value is usually low. Upgrading traditional industries and moving towards the mid-to-high position in the value chain is key to China's manufacturing sector transitioning from quantity to quality. International standards should be applied to manufacturing processes. New technologies, such as the Internet, big data, and artificial intelligence should be further integrated into the real economy as we promote an advanced manufacturing sector, and build world-class manufacturing clusters. It is also necessary to develop a modern service industry.

A dynamic balance between supply and demand is essential. For some time now, excessive investment in particular industries have led to excess capacity beyond the actual needs of society. Capacity reduction measures taken over the past years have produced tangible results. In 2016 alone, the steel industry reduced capacity by over 65 million tons, while the coal industry reduced by 290 million tons. However, a lot more remains to be done in these key industries and other industries with excess capacity, and that requires much determination. It will further contribute to optimizing resource allocation and improving supply-demand balance.

INNOVATION AS A NEW GROWTH DRIVER

On October 10, 2017, the National Astronomical Observatories of the Chinese Academy of Sciences published an exciting piece of news -- China's "Sky Eye" telescope had discovered six new pulsars in the Milky Way. This was the first such discovery made using Chinese astronomical equipment, marking a breakthrough for China in this area and receiving strong acclaim from the international astronomical community. In recent years, as a matter of fact, there has been no lack of excitement in China's innovation: the launch of the Hard X-ray Modulation Telescope, also known as "Insight"; the debut of the first Chinese-built aircraft carrier and commercial jetliner C919; and China's leading position in quantum communication technology. The ancient Chinese fairy tale of flying to the sky to catch the moon and diving to the depths of the ocean to catch the turtle villain is becoming a reality.

Today China ranks among the most advanced in key areas such as aviation, medicine, biological research, and information technology. As technological advances contribute more to its economic growth each year, China has become a major technology powerhouse. However, we should also clearly realize that overall China still falls far behind world leaders in many areas.

Globally, a new revolution in technology and industry is emerging. IT, biotechnologies, new materials and new energy solutions, etc., are increasingly being applied. Technological innovation has become a battlefield for major competitors, and whoever excels in technological innovation will win the battle. Innovation is the number-one driving force for development and provides strategic support for a modern economy, so it is in response to this

Sky Eye Telescope

changing world that the 19th CPC National Congress outlined a new strategy on innovation to seal China's place among the world's best.

Basic research. As the source of technological innovation, basic research must receive more attention. It is an important indicator of a country's core competitiveness. As China's economy and technology grow, it needs to import more advanced technologies, but in fact, money cannot buy either critical or core technologies. That is why we need to increase basic research and expand key national-level technology projects, in order to make breakthroughs in frontier technologies, modern engineering technologies, and game-changing, disruptive innovations, among others. This will propel China to preeminence in science and technology.

A framework that encourages innovation. Innovation is, so to speak, a system engineering project that involves the government, companies, universities,

"Gazelle Enterprises" in China

"Gazelle enterprises" refer to companies that have crossed the "valley of death", the most vulnerable early stage of a start-up, and entered a high-growth period. These enterprises are characterized by rapid growth, strong innovation, new specializations, and expansion potential. According to a national report issued jointly by the Torch Center of the Ministry of Science and Technology and Great Wall Strategy Consultants in November 2017, there were 2,567 "gazelle enterprises" in China's hi-tech zones in 2016, an increase of 491 over the previous year, and the "gazelle rate" reached 2.75 percent, compared with less than 2 percent in most other countries. The photo shows a display of products from Xiaomi, Inc.

---

developing top-level research universities and institutes, and creating favorable conditions for innovative industry leaders.

An institutional framework for science and technology. Technological innovation and institutional reform are like the wings of bird or wheels of a vehicle: when they operate together innovative potential can be unleashed.

The 2017 National Science and Technology Awards

On January 8, 2018, the National Science and Technology Awards Ceremony was held in Beijing. A total of 271 projects and 9 scientists were selected as the winners. Two individuals won the highest Science and Technology Award. Of the 35 National Natural Science Awards, 2 were first prizes and 33 second prizes. Of the 66 National Technology Invention Awards, 4 were first prizes and 62 second prizes. Of the 170 National Science and Technology Progress Awards, 3 were special prizes, 21 first prizes, and 146 second prizes. Seven international scientists were granted the China International Science and Technology Cooperation Award. The photo is an overview of the National Science and Technology Awards Ceremony.

and research institutes working together in a highly efficient system of innovation. In recent years, there has been substantial progress in setting up such a framework, contributing significantly to advancement in technology. One estimate put China's innovation index score for 2016 at 181.2, representing an increase of 5.7 percent from 2015. Measures should include establishing national laboratories in key areas, building vital technological infrastructure,

The Global Hard Technology Innovation Conference

In November 2017, the Global Hard Technology Innovation Conference was held in China. The conference covered key hard technology areas such as AI, aviation, biotechnology, optoelectronic chips, IT, new materials, new energy, and smart manufacturing. The goal of the conference was to build a "Belt and Road" platform for cooperation and sharing of technological innovation. It attracted top hard technology experts and products from around the world, and was a forum to showcase Chinese brands. The photo shows the Global Hard Technology Innovation Conference.

The present sci-tech institutional framework needs to change by putting in place mechanisms that serve the innovation process. This means creating an enabling market environment, protecting intellectual property rights, better funding and financing mechanisms, an effective distribution network, and a plan for training, hiring and managing talent. A market-oriented framework will allow businesses to play a major role in technological innovation and create synergy between business and academia.

RURAL REVITALIZATION

At the Central Conference on Agriculture held in Beijing, December 28-29, 2017, General Secretary Xi Jinping reviewed the historic achievements and reforms since 2012 in rural development, agriculture and the wellbeing of the rural population, commonly referred to as the "three rural issues". He emphasized the importance of a rural revitalization strategy and laid out its guidelines.

It can be said that the wellbeing of its farmers reflects a nation's prosperity. The weakest link in China's national development lies in its rural areas. A thriving agriculture provides a solid foundation for rural stability and improves the wellbeing of the farmers, which in turn contributes to prosperity across the land. Effectively addressing the "three rural issues" and coordinating development in town and countryside will bring prosperity to both, thus ensuring success in building a moderately prosperous society before we embark on the next leg towards a modern socialist country.

In recent years, agricultural and rural development have topped the CPC and government agenda. Each calendar year, the very first document issued by the CPC Central Committee always focuses on agriculture, and proposes initiatives to address the "three rural issues". Harvests have been good for years in a row, and rural standards of living are up, with farmers' annual per-capita disposable income now over 12,000 RMB. The rural revitalization strategy has helped develop businesses, created a pleasant living environment, promoted better social relationships and effective governance, and injected new vigor into the countryside. This has benefited millions of rural residents.

Agricultural modernization must be accelerated. Without it overall modernization is impossible. Currently, agricultural and rural development remains the weak link in our overall modernization process, which calls for synchronized industrialization, IT application, urbanization and modernization of agriculture. That is why priority must be given to agricultural and rural development, which means setting up a modern agro-business system, promoting farming techniques and management expertise as part of a distinctly Chinese socialist model for rural revitalization.

Pilot programs for modern agriculture

In recent years, Wudi County in Shandong Province has taken the initiative in setting up demonstration gardens to promote modern, green, high-yield, and efficient agricultural methods. A total of 71 such gardens have been built in the county, effectively promoting the coordinated and healthy development of up-to-date techniques. In the photo staff of the Modern Agricultural Science Pilot Program at Shuiwan Township are cleaning the roots of hydroponic vegetables.

Rural reform must continue. Forty years ago, our reforms first started in the rural areas and led to profound changes across the land. As we enter the new age, reform is once again reviving the countryside. Continuous reforms are needed in the land tenure and collective ownership systems, as well as continued support for agriculture.Policies and mechanisms to encourage integrated urban-rural development will offer further incentives to farmers to tap agricultural potential and boost rural development.

Army veterans become Party secretaries

Over the last few years, the city of Dazhou in Sichuan Province has carefully selected over 170 young army veterans, Party members with solid political and professional credentials, to work as Party secretaries in some of the poorest, most backward villages facing the toughest poverty eradication challenges. In the photo one of the Party secretaries is helping a villager harvest farm-grown crayfish.

More talent for the countryside. As China's urbanization accelerates, cities have seen a large influx of migrant workers from the countryside. Many villages have been almost completely "emptied out". There is an urgent need for people who can take the lead in reinvigorating the countryside, people who understand farming, like village life, and care about the farmers. This is a huge undertaking offering an abundance of opportunities for aspiring individuals to realize their full potential. Support measures are needed to encourage migrant workers to return home to work or start their own business. Incentives will be offered to encourage talent flows to rural areas. Also important is the selection of competent administrators, including college graduates, to be village Party secretaries or assume other responsible positions. Effective training should be provided to rural officials, who should be given appropriate responsibilities; farmers too need more coaching and training in new techniques and entrepreneurship. Such measures are aimed at creating an environment where agriculture and farming become attractive and promising professions, and the countryside an ideal place to call home.

COORDINATED REGIONAL DEVELOPMENT

On April 1, 2017, just at the start of spring, the CPC Central Committee announced a new strategy crucial for the new millennium: the decision to create Xiongan New Area. The news reverberated across the country, and soon became a hot topic, both at home and abroad. To put it in perspective, this decision is a brilliant move for enhancing the coordinated regional development of Beijing and Tianjin municipalities with Hebei Province. It is a "millennium strategy" of historic significance.

In recent years, a number of vast regional development plans have been proceeding apace: the development of the West, the revitalization of the Northeast, the rise of Central China, the continuing lead of the East, and the catch-up development of former revolutionary base areas, ethnic minority areas, and remote and impoverished areas. Coordinated regional development is in good shape. However, we must admit that uneven development and large regional differences still persist. The Guidelines for Coordinated Regional Development unveiled at the 19th CPC National Congress provide strategic and long-term solutions for these problems.

Coordinated regional development can be compared to a symphony orchestra. China is a vast country where development levels and conditions vary substantially from place to place. The four main development "plates" of Western, Northeast, Central and Eastern China must continue their growth and progress as they constitute the principal configuration of our national

The 2017 China Marine Economy Expo

From December 14 to 17, 2017, the China Marine Economy Expo was held in the city of Zhanjiang in Guangdong Province. The theme was "A blue path to innovative development". Some 3,000 domestic and international companies from 63 countries and regions came to exhibit their products. In the photo is a model of the vessel used in the first pilot project for extracting "combustible ice" in Chinese territorial waters.

development. In the meantime, the functional zone strategy should continue at full steam, and there will be increased support for other places such as former revolutionary base areas, areas inhabited by ethnic minorities, and remote and economically disadvantaged areas. In this regional collaborative "symphony", no one plays on a whim but rather contributes to the whole piece. That is why a regional coordination system is crucial to ensuring a seamless interface between all these disparate regions, playing the "symphony" of developing in step with each other.

Just as a vocal ensemble needs a lead singer, development efforts need a lead contributor. Modern economic history shows that economic growth in core areas radiates out to surrounding areas and pushes them forward too. Examples include the cluster of cities in the Great Lakes region of North America, the Core Cities Group of UK and the Kanto Economic Zone of Japan. In China too, a number of centers that drive regional growth have emerged in key areas and city clusters, such as the Beijing-Tianjin-Hebei Urban Agglomeration, the Yangtze River Economic Zone, the Guangdong-Hong Kong-Macao Greater Bay Area, the Chengdu-Chongqing Metropolitan Area, the Central Plains Economic Region, and the Harbin-Changchun Metropolitan Area. A future focus will be to rationalize the division of work and functions within the city clusters themselves so that they can lead the way in institutional innovation, sci-tech advancement, and industrial upgrading, and thus drive coordinated development in the regions around them.

An integrated land-ocean strategy for national development. History shows that a nation's capacity to use the oceans is key to its prosperity and an important factor in its national strength. China covers over 9.6 million square kilometers of land and has over 3 million square kilometers of territorial waters. The 21st century is the "maritime century" and China has made the strategic decision to become a maritime power. This is in line with global trends, which will provide space for its development and give it more global influence. We are ready to embrace the oceans, to build greater prosperity and to pursue an integrated land-ocean development strategy to ensure harmony between man and the seas.

China's economic development is at a critical juncture. There are many obstacles to overcome in our efforts to build a modern economy that will propel us into a new and more prosperous future.

Deliberate choices for new imperatives

He Lifeng (Party Secretary and Minister, the National Development and Reform Commission): China's economic development is already transitioning from high-speed growth to a greater focus on quality. Blind pursuit of speed and scale is no longer a sustainable option. The effects of the international financial crisis continue to be felt, and global economic recovery is still bumpy. China must switch to quality economic development in order to withstand fierce international competition. Building a modern economy means making deliberate choices to change to a new vision of development that relies on innovation and economic breakthroughs to achieve quality and efficiency.

Quality for sustained healthy economic development

The Central Economic Work Conference met in Beijing from December 18 to 20 in 2017. It was pointed out at the conference that as socialism with Chinese characteristics is now in a new era, so is the country's economic development. The defining feature of this transition is a shift from high-speed growth to one that focuses on quality. This is in response to new economic imperatives: maintaining sustained healthy development, addressing different important social challenges, completing the process of building a moderately prosperous society, and moving towards a modern socialist country.

Now and in the coming years, this focus on quality will determine our thinking on development, our economic policies and macro-economic controls. It is imperative to formulate as quickly as possible the corresponding indicators, policies, standards, and statistical systems. Also needed are mechanisms for outcome and performance evaluation. Such measures will improve the institutional environment and facilitate China's economic shift towards quality.

Q & A

Q: What are "the five priority measures"?

A: "The five priority measures" are part of supply-side structural reforms, including: capacity reduction, destocking, deleveraging, cost reduction, and fixing weaknesses. The aim is to achieve a dynamic balance between supply and demand by cutting back on oversupply and satisfying demand.

CHAPTER 8

CHOOSING THE RIGHT SYSTEM FOR THE COUNTRY

—Building a political system based on popular participation

D emocracy is the lifeline of socialism. Without democracy, there would be no socialism, and there would be no modernization or national renewal to speak of. The more advanced socialism is, the more vibrant democracy becomes. We must keep to the path of political development under socialism with Chinese characteristics, and strengthen the system based on popular participation as we continue to advance socialism with Chinese characteristics with greater democracy and political progress.

A POLITICAL SYSTEM THAT MUST BE UPHELD

"Little beans in our hands, and they are votes we cast with care. Choose good people who do good things and we will be in good hands." This was a simple rhyme that described the process of election in villages in the Shaanxi-Gansu-Ningxia Border Region during the War of Resistance Against Japanese Aggression from the mid-1930s till 1945. Using soya beans to vote for the people they wanted to choose as their leaders, the villagers demonstrated a desire to have a say on issues that mattered to their lives. When Huang Yanpei, a celebrated public figure of the time, visited Yan'an in July 1945, he was very impressed with what was happening there, and expressed the hope that the Communist Party of China could find a new system that would work. In response, Mao Zedong said that they had found it, and that was democracy. If the government was put under the watch of the people, it would not dare to rest on its laurels. As long as people were involved in the process, the government would not fail.

The political system a country adopts and the path it takes for its political development are determined by the country's specific conditions as well as its history and culture. They must happen in the right country with the right conditions. Socialist democracy with Chinese characteristics is not just another version of traditional Chinese political systems, nor is it a replica of Western-style democracy. Rather, it is an original creation developed through years of search, trial, and practice. It has unparalleled advantages and distinctive features and it is the right way for China. It has been proven in practice time and again that it is a political path that works well for the country.

It is the right way because it is a system led by the Communist Party of China, based on the participation of the people, and governed by the rule of law. The CPC plays the leading role in this process to ensure that people have their say and that the rule of law is observed. The participation of the people in the decision-making process is the very purpose of the system, and without it, there would be no basis for either the CPC's leadership or the rule of law. Further, the rule of law serves as a safeguard in that without it, there would be no legal guarantee for the leadership of the CPC or the participation of the people. Those three components – the CPC leadership, the participation of the people, and the rule of law – form an organic whole in which each piece depends on the others. Each component plays a distinct role in ensuring that the CPC exercises effective leadership, the power of the country rests with the people, and democracy is institutionalized and enshrined in the legal system. Thus, political activities in China are robust, stable, and orderly.

It is the right way because it is an ideal combination of electoral and consultative democracy. We emphasize the role of electoral democracy in which people exercise their rights through elections. At the same time, we also make sure that people are part of the decision-making process through consultative democracy. Through the involvement of the people by both of those means, democracy is ensured both procedurally and on its results, in both form and substance.

It is the right way because it is both efficient and carefully scrutinized. The Chinese democracy is highly efficient in the sense that decision-making is quick and well-informed and is followed by effective implementation. At the same time, however, there are scrutiny mechanisms in place to prevent the abuse of power. We therefore have a system in which power is exercised with efficiency, under careful supervision, in a way that can help avoid problems associated with the extreme centralization of power. It also overcomes the disadvantages of Western-style democracy, in which state power is fragmented, the society lacks cohesion, and the government is weak.

Just as no two leaves on a tree are the same, no two political models in the world are identical. A political system cannot exist in isolation from the country's specific socio-political conditions, history, or culture. It cannot claim to be the system of choice for everyone, nor should it be copied after a model from other countries. In the new era, we must keep to the path of political development under socialism with Chinese characteristics, with steady efforts to strengthen popular participation and push for reforms in our political system. We will thus ensure that the people are fully involved, in different forms and ways, in the decision-making process concerning state affairs, the economy, culture, and the society.

AN EFFECTIVE PEOPLE'S CONGRESS SYSTEM

On September 15, 1954, the First National People's Congress (NPC) of the People's Republic of China held its first session at Huairen Hall in Zhongnanhai, the center of Beijing. More than 1,200 delegates from different parts of the country representing 600 million Chinese people gathered in Beijing to deliberate on issues relating to the country's future development. That event marked the beginning of the people's congress system nationwide and a new era for the democracy of the people in China. The event was widely celebrated in newspapers at the time, with commentary like "an opportunity for the Chinese people that has never been seen before!", "this is a day to celebrate!", and "a joyous day for the Chinese people!"

More than 60 years have passed since then, and with maturity and confidence, the people's congress system has covered a lot of ground to become the robust deliberative system it is today. In March each year, delegates meet during the regular session of the National People's Congress in the Great Hall of the People in Beijing to exercise their power on behalf of the people, an event that has become an important part of China's political life. Sixty years of experience has fully proved that the people's congress is the right system for China as a socialist country with its specific conditions. It is a system that guarantees the people's participation in the decision-making process and provides a solid foundation for national renewal. It is an important part of China's political institutions.

Delegates attending the first meeting of the First National People's Congress, 1954

So what kind of a system is it? It is a fundamental and effective political system implemented under the leadership of the CPC, based on popular participation and the rule of law. According to the Chinese constitution, all power in the People's Republic of China belongs to the people, which is exercised through the National People's Congress and people's congresses at local levels. The National People's Congress is the highest body of state power, and local people's congresses hold a similar status for the various localities. The late Chairman Mao Zedong once described the importance of the people's congress system with an analogy: "The NPC is like a buddha with huge

Mobile ballot boxes to facilitate voting in Hefei, Anhui Province

In addition to setting up 352 polling stations, the district government of Yaohai in Hefei, Anhui Province provided 247 mobile ballot boxes, which were taken to the homes of voters with limited mobility to make sure they could fully exercise their political right and choose their representatives to the people's congress. Pictured here are voting station staff members collecting ballots with mobile ballot boxes.

hands, and we can't jump out of his hands. We must follow all NPC decisions, since the president and the premier are elected by the NPC."

How does the people's congress ensure the effective exercise of power by the people? To determine if a country has a democratic political system, the most important thing to look at is not a fanfare of elections, but whether the will of the people is fully represented and whether their interests are effectively protected. Delegates to the NPC and the local people's congresses are elected through democratic processes. They are accountable to the people and overseen by the people. The system as such is a fundamental guarantee that that the people are truly the masters of the country. The report of the 19th CPC National Congress emphasized: "We must provide the support and assurance that the people exercise state power through the people's congresses," and that "people's congresses exercise their powers of legislation, supervision, decision-making, and appointment and removal of government officials." As the people's congress system continues to improve, it will serve as a more effective institution for the people to be involved in running the country.

How does the people's congress system ensure through law the participation by the people? Law is the basic rule that must be followed for anything and everything in this land. The rule of law is the very foundation of the CPC as it leads the people in running the country, and it is an important instrument to ensure the exercise of power by the people. The Constitution is the basic law of the land and the foundation of governance. It is a representation of the collective will of the Party and the people. An important function of the National People's Congress and its Standing Committee is to supervise the implementation of the Constitution, safeguard its supremacy and authority, and ensure its sanctity and inviolability. Good laws are the foundation of good governance, and they serve as a mirror in reflecting public opinion. The people's congresses at all levels have a paramount role to play in legislation as they make, amend, revoke, or interpret the law. They provide a process in which law is made on an informed basis, through democratic and legal procedures, and every law is made on the basis of the Constitution and the will and support of the people.

THE ADVANTAGES OF THE CONSULTATIVE DEMOCRATIC PROCESS

In January 1979, in the cold winter of Beijing, Deng Xiaoping invited Hu Juewen, Hu Ziang, Rong Yiren, Gu Gengyu and Zhou Shutao to a meeting at the Great Hall of the People. The five senior business leaders sat down with Deng Xiaoping and, over a hotpot lunch, discussed the role of business and industry in the country's drive towards modernization. This was the famed story of "five elders having a hotpot lunch at the Great Hall of the People",

The first meeting of the Chinese People's Political Consultative Conference, 1949

which was actually one of the many consultations that the CPC conducted with people from all walks of life. Since the CPC's 18th National Congress in 2012, the National Committee of the Chinese People's Political Consultative Conference (CPPCC) has been holding bi-weekly consultation meetings, which have become an important and well-received form of consultative democracy.

Socialist consultative democracy is a creation of the CPC and the Chinese people. In September 1949, the first plenary session of the CPPCC adopted the "Common Program of the Chinese People's Political Consultative Conference" and the "Organizational Law of the Chinese People's Political Consultative Conference", which marked the birth of a system for multi-party cooperation and political consultation under the leadership of the CPC. For more than 60 years, the CPPCC has been an important part of the country's progress, making concerted and positive efforts to contribute to the cause of socialist modernization.

Past and present experiences have repeatedly proven that consultative democracy is an effective democratic process in the Chinese context. Under the system of socialism with Chinese characteristics, it provides a vehicle for extensive discussions, through which the highest possible degree of agreement and consensus can be reached on issues close to the hearts and minds of the people. In a large country with an enormous population, there are always issues that are complicated and interests that need to be balanced. It is therefore particularly important to hold consultations before any major decisions are made.

Consultative democracy takes place extensively in China's political activities in different areas and on various issues. There are consultations carried out by and among political parties, by people's congresses, government agencies, CPPCC national and local committees, and with associations, communities, and civil societies, covering a wide range of issues in economy, politics, culture, society, environment, and party-building. They take different forms, such as issue-specific consultations, counterpart consultations, cross-sector consultations, and consultations on proposals to be submitted or having already been submitted to the people's congress or CPPCC. There are also mechanisms in place for these consultations including seminars, talks, stakeholder meetings, hearings, and so on. Such a comprehensive and multi-level institutional arrangement ensures the maximum participation of the people in political activities.

In the new era of socialism with Chinese characteristics, consultative democracy has become even more essential. The 19th CPC National Congress proposed goals for consultative democracy to play a more important role, with improved institutions and procedures and effective implementation, to

Legal-themed parks to foster a culture of respect for the law

In recent years, permanent exhibitions in public parks in some cities have become an innovative way to promote a culture of respect for the rule of law. Texts of laws and regulations highly relevant to people's lives are displaced in showcases, on display screens or embedded in the landscape to raise awareness of the rule of law and create a microenvironment that encourages citizens to learn about the law as they enjoy public places. Pictured here is a snapshot of Guangji Park in Gusu District, Suzhou, Jiangsu Province.

ensure broad and continuous participation in the political process. As an advisory body, the CPPCC provides an important channel for consultative democracy. This is the approach it must follow as it conducts political consultations, provides oversight on the work of the government, and advises on state affairs. Consultative democracy must be further improved in both substance and form in order to build consensus and unity.

STRENGTHENING THE RULE OF LAW FOR THE COUNTRY'S GOVERNANCE

A country becomes strong when laws are observed. To become fully modern, a country must be based on the rule of law. As China moves towards modernization, it must implement law-based governance as a necessary condition for socialist democracy to grow, and a strong foundation for achieving modernization and the Chinese dream of national renewal.

Important work is being done on the rule of law in order to improve the country's legal structure and promote law-based governance. Since the 18th CPC National Congress, there have been unprecedented efforts to promote the rule of law as part of a "four-pronged comprehensive strategy". In particular, the Fourth Plenary Session of the 18th CPC Central Committee, held in 2014, decided on goals and a roadmap for achieving law-based governance, accelerating the pace of reform, and bringing forward promising prospects for the country on the basis of the rule of law.

A new chapter started at the 19th National Congress when the CPC further emphasized the importance of building the rule of law as a revolutionary process to transform the country's governance and thereby ensure the continued development of socialism with Chinese characteristics and the long-term viability of the CPC and the country. We will make greater efforts to build a legal system that serves as the bedrock for the country, the government, and the society. It is a system in which the rule of law is followed in everything we do, from governance to law enforcement to administrative proceedings.

We must foster respect for law. People must hold respect for the law and believe in it. They must have a strong awareness of laws before they can voluntarily observe them and abide by them in their daily lives. The authority of the law derives from the support and recognition afforded to it by the people. It is therefore imperative to increase the awareness of the law and build a culture of respect for the rule of law, in which the supremacy of the Constitution and the authority of the law are observed, and everyone is equal before the law. The respect for law should be found in legislation, law enforcement, justice, and in our daily lives. We should live in a society where abiding by the law is a matter of honor and pride and breaking the law brings shame.

We must continue legal reforms, which provide the impetus for the building of the rule of law. Important progress has been made in legal reform since the 18th CPC National Congress, and profound changes have been made in various areas. For instance, there have been increased efforts to make better-quality laws, to enforce laws on well-defined procedures, to administer laws with fairness and justice, and to carry out more effective campaigns to enhance awareness of the law. As reform moves into the most important and difficult stage, we must focus our efforts on key areas to achieve results that can be replicated in other areas. With these efforts underway, we will be able to bring about more progress in the reform of the judicial system and the administrative law-enforcement system.

We must continue to work on implementation. Building the rule of law is like building a large house. Now that we have the blueprint, the construction can start. We must lay a solid foundation and build from the ground up. The 19th CPC National Congress presented plans for building law-based governance and identified goals for implementing the rule of law, with a number of new initiatives to support legal reforms and respond to the changing times. To achieve these goals, we must adopt a systematic approach with targeted measures in specific areas. Ultimately, our efforts in sound lawmaking, stringent law enforcement, fairness in the administration of justice, and universal observance of the law will bear the fruit we seek.

Keep to the path we have chosen. This is the conclusion China has reached on the basis of changes, setbacks, and difficulties it has experienced in its history. Political development under socialism with Chinese characteristics is the route we have chosen after decades of exploration and hardship. We are justified in what we seek and confident in our ability to achieve further successes in the future, contributing Chinese wisdom to the political progress of humankind along the way.

The path for political development under socialism with Chinese characteristics: an inevitable choice

Shen Chunyao (Chairman of Legislative Affairs Commission of the Standing Committee of the National People's Congress)

The path for political development under socialism with Chinese characteristics is the result of years of search and experiments as the CPC applied the fundamental principles of Marxism in the Chinese context. It is the result of profound changes of a hundred years in Chinese modern history, especially for the past four decades of reform and opening up. It is the inevitable choice that the Chinese people made as they took their future into their own hands on their journey towards prosperity.

Q&A

Q: What is the biweekly consultation meeting?

A: It is a biweekly consultation mechanism established by the 12th National Committee of the CPPCC on the basis of the CPPCC's earlier practices. The meeting is held every other week and the first such meeting was convened on October 22, 2013. The meetings are usually organized by CPPCC special committees with designated topics for each meeting. The meetings bring together people across different sectors to engage in detailed discussions of specific issues high on the agenda of the CPC and the government and issues that attract widespread public attention. These events are a reflection of the dual role of the CPPCC as a major channel for consultative democracy as well as a consultation mechanism in itself.

Socialist consultative democracy has its unique advantages.

Meng Xiangfeng (Executive Deputy Secretary of the Work Committee of the Departments under the CPC Central Committee and Deputy Director of the General Office of the CPC Central Committee)

Socialist consultative democracy has several unique advantages: first, it is a process through which the broadest possible consensus can be reached for decision making and implementation, as it helps avoid the pitfalls of competition and even conflict that would otherwise arise as political and interest groups jostle for their own gains; second, it makes sure that all interests and needs are considered in the decision making process, which helps prevent impasse and exclusion as a result of fighting among political factions; third, it serves as a broad-based mechanism for identifying and rectifying missteps to avoid ill-informed decisions; fourth, it allows the people to have their voice heard and participate in governance at all levels; fifth, it can bring together people's insights and efforts to help advance the reform agenda and make sure policies are made with the broadest possible support and work is effectively performed.

CHAPTER 9

CULTIVATING THE CHINESE SPIRIT IN A NEW ERA

—Fostering a culture based on socialist values

In the summer of 2017, *Wolf Warrior II*, a Chinese-produced movie sequel broke the box office record of the year to become an immediate cultural phenomenon in China. It was a well-produced awe-inspiring film featuring justice fighters and bursting with patriotic pride. The film was just one example of the many top-notch cultural products that have become ever more creative, widely disseminated and influential in the past few years, in a country with a vibrant culture.

Culture is the foundation of national strength. It is the soul of a country and its people, and the life force behind the development and progress of a society. For a nation to revitalize itself, it takes inner strength in addition to material conditions. In this regard, our national renewal requires unwavering commitment to a development path that focuses on fostering a culture of socialism with Chinese characteristics and building a socialist cultural powerhouse, to create the intellectual power for national renewal.

BUILDING CONFIDENCE IN OUR CULTURE

Over 2,000 years ago, Confucius toured the various kingdoms making up what is now China with his disciples. Two millennia later, stories of these trips -- now a part of China's fondest memories -- have become embodied in an eponymous institute with a global presence. With over 500 establishments in 146 countries and regions and over 2.3 million students, the Confucius Institute is a window on Chinese culture and a hallmark of China's cultural confidence.

What does it mean to have confidence in our culture? In a nutshell, it means confidence in the values and vitality of the Chinese culture as something that provides enduring support to social development. Confidence in our culture matters for the future of the nation, the survival of our culture, and the independence of our national ethos. A nation that ignores or rejects its

Confucius Institute: a window on Chinese culture

The Confucius Institute is a non-profit organization with the mission to teach the Chinese language and Chinese culture overseas. Its most important function is providing standard and authentic resources for teaching Chinese and a formal channel for learning Chinese. Since the establishment of a pilot institute in the Uzbek capital of Tashkent on June 15, 2004, over 500 more have sprouted up throughout the world. Pictured here is the 12th Confucius Institute Conference held in Xi'an, Shaanxi Province, December 2017.

own culture will have a bleak future and is likely to allow its past tragedies to repeat themselves.

The uniqueness of our socialist culture with Chinese characteristics is rooted in the fact that it is time-honored, tempered by fire and enriched with tested truths. It is one of the most resilient, meaningful and dynamic cultures. Thus, confidence in our culture is grounded in reality and in our vitality.

Confidence in our culture is rooted in our history. The Chinese culture is ancient as it is sophisticated, with 5,000 years of history played out over a vast span of territory, producing numerous influential philosophers from Confucius to Wang Yangming and bequeathing to future generations a rich cultural and literary legacy. Ancient yet vibrant, China boasts of the only uninterrupted civilization in the world. Our civilization is the hallmark of our ethos and the progenitor of our culture, standing strong through centuries of trials and tribulations and shining like a bright star in the galaxy of human civilizations. History is the solid foundation on which we find confidence in our culture.

Our confidence comes from fighting and winning against all odds. As a Chinese saying goes, in the deadly cold winter blooms the sweetest flower. The appeal of our culture comes from revolutionary and socialist roots nurtured with blood, sweat and tears shed in our long-standing struggles. The spirit of our culture gave inspiration to the founding of the Chinese Communist Party, guided the epic Long March, and led us through the turbulent waters in the early days of revolution. It is embodied in the selflessness of our national role models, such as Lei Feng and Wang Jinxi. It has propelled us to win victories in the most difficult circumstances, whether making breakthroughs in outer space explorations, fighting natural disasters or transforming deserts into forests. This spirit is the life force of our revolution and reform, the manifestation of the creativity of the CPC and the people, and the bedrock of our confidence.

Our confidence comes from successes we have scored. Shortly after the founding of the People's Republic, Chairman Mao Zedong predicted "a cultural boom that is bound to take place as the economy reaches its heyday," and his prediction is coming true. Since the launch of the reform and opening up policy, our distinctly Chinese socialism has been gaining traction. It has enriched our philosophical thinking, fine-tuned our institutional framework, and created the China miracle. It has thus enhanced the appeal of the socialist culture and provided a basis on which our cultural confidence is anchored.

Culture is the expression of our convictions and the glue that holds us together. Building a country with a robust socialist culture was identified as one of our goals for a new era at the 19th CPC National Congress, along with guiding principles and a roadmap to this end. This process must be guided by Marx's teachings to ensure that culture and the arts are at the service of the people and society in a diverse and inclusive environment. This is key to the creative transformation and innovative development we need in order to create new cultural glory and bring about the national renewal.

REAFFIRMING THE CPC'S LEADERSHIP

Ideology determines the nature of a culture and the direction of its development, and is therefore its heart and soul. It is key to the survival of a political party or a nation. According to Karl Marx, an era can end when its prevailing ideology crumbles. Indeed, lessons abound in history and present times showing that the unraveling of a political system usually starts with the erosion of its political and philosophical guidelines, leading to the dissolution of its other defenses.

Throught history, ideology has always been an important item in the toolbox for statesmen around the world. It shapes a nation's identity, shows the way forward, and provides political safeguards. The CPC has always attached great importance to promoting political awareness and has been effective in implementing measures in this regard. In the extraordinary journey from revolution to reform, political awareness has played a critical role in galvanizing and guiding action and sustaining national cohesion. After the 18th CPC National Congress in 2012, in particular, a healthier, more optimistic and vibrant political landscape emerged, with recurring themes conveying positive messages that boost morale and prod us to march in unison towards our goal. Applause on social media follows: "Never before have we ever been so united as one people with a strong desire to create a better future."

Diverse values and competing views have emerged out of a complex domestic and international context, particularly accompanying the profound changes sweeping across the society. Ideological conflict is ongoing and multidimensional, and we cannot afford to ignore what is at stake. There is no place for complacency or a false sense of security; we must keep our eyes peeled and ears pricked. The CPC's leadership on the political front must be strengthened. More robust and effective measures should be taken to this end and unite our people with shared ideals, values and moral standards.

The 2017 Media Integration and Development Forum held in Shenzhen

With the theme "We Are One", the forum, held on August 19, 2017 in the city of Shenzhen, Guangdong Province, boasted over 500 participants, representing different departments and agencies of the central government, local government communications offices, national and local journalists, Internet business executives, experts and scholars. Pictured here is the inauguration ceremony of the Integrated Media Platform Institute set up by the People's Daily with several other institutions held during the forum.

It is always crucial to find where our anchor is. Theoretical guidance underpins political decisions. Marxism provides the fundamental guidance for the CPC and the country, and is the lodestar and soul of the socialist thinking. Xi Jinping Thought on Socialism with Chinese Characteristics for a New Era embodies what we have achieved by adapting Marxism to China's realities. We must remain committed to this guiding theory, which inspires and empowers the CPC and the people as they move in unison towards the future.

Steady leadership is essential when it comes to political guidance. Proper guidance will place the country and the people on the right track, while wrong guidance can lead to disasters. Strong leadership on theoretical issues ensures proper guidance that defines the path forward clearly. Effective and consistent guidance is needed for different areas, including theoretical studies, journalism, publishing, literary and art creation, and promotion of ethical standards, especially against the backdrop of a fast evolving media landscape. The reach and influence of the media depends on its ability to innovate and to get the message across effectively. In order to become the source of proper guidance, the media needs enhanced communication channels and creative input. For this purpose, efforts will be made to promote media convergence and build a diverse group of flagship media outlets that are competitive, credible, and use cutting-edge technologies.

PROMOTING CORE VALUES

The Chinese society has never been in want of role models. Examples in recent years include Gong Quanzhen, who dedicated all her life to rural education; Huang Xuhua, who designed China's first nuclear submarine; Liao Junbo, a county Party secretary and an exemplar public servant; Huang Dafa, who accomplished the impossible by building an aqueduct to transform a remote village; Zhang Lili, who risked her own life to keep her students out of harm's way; Wu Bin, a bus driver who died saving the 24 passengers aboard; Liu Hongan, a college-grad-turned-food-vendor who refuses to sell unsafe food, and Jia Liqun, a pediatrician renowned for his skill and dedication. Examples such as the above inspire people in all walks of life and speak volumes about our moral strength. What these ordinary folks have done reflects our core socialist values and the true spirit of contemporary China.

Values are a moral compass that guides our action. Generally accepted values are the glue that holds a society and a nation together. At the heart of these are core values, which are the lifeblood of a nation and the theoretical and moral foundation of a country.

"100 Talks on Core Values"

Experts, scholars and role models have been invited to share their insights and real life stories in a lecture series, which were disseminated through online video streaming, online and offline interactions and newspaper reports. After its kick-off at Renmin University on May 30, 2014, the lecture series had featured 67 guest speakers by the end of 2017. Pictured here is the 50th lecture held in Yuncheng, Shanxi Province.

In present-day China, core socialist values embody our national ethos and represent the moral aspirations of all people. Since its 18th National Congress, the CPC Central Committee has repeatedly emphasized the importance of fostering core socialist values and undertaken key initiatives in this regard. Enthusiastic participation by officials at all levels and the general public has created strong momentum for the advancement of core socialist values.

Cultivating core socialist values is a gradual, open-ended process that focuses

Zhangjiagang, Jiangsu Province: Integrating Ethics in Urban-Rural Development

In recent years, the city of Zhangjiagang in Jiangsu Province has become well known for its transformation into a showcase for economic prosperity and ethical living. The city owes its success to its efforts to foster core socialist values. It was the first nationally recognized ethics model town and went on to hold the title for three more consecutive years. Pictured here is a part of the city.

on the inner world. It is a task that has grown in importance and urgency as we open a new chapter in our journey.

Education is essential. An old saying tells us that the customs of a nation are not immutable; they can be changed through education. Education lays the groundwork for change. It provides guidance, builds awareness, and instills core socialist values in our people. In response to the need to strengthen ethical standards, measures to promote core values should be integrated into civic education, ethical education, and culture creation, production and dissemination. We should take full advantage of the power of new communication tools such as Weibo (microblogging), WeChat (messaging and social media), micro videos and micro movies to package and convey moral messages in a way that is widely accessible and compelling so that they can be internalized.

It is important to translate values into behaviors, which is always easier said than done. To cultivate core socialist values and translate them into behaviors, we must make them relevant to people's daily lives in ways as concrete and practical as possible. These values will then become a part of who we are and putting them into action will become second nature. Major commemorative days or traditional holidays provide opportunities for people to learn to appreciate the essence of these values. We can take advantage of these occasions to organize themed activities or events such as flag raising ceremonies and induction ceremonies that welcome new members into the CPC, the Youth League or the Young Pioneers. Civility and ethical behavior should be promoted in cities, villages, schools, workplaces and family life. Character-building activities will be organized to celebrate the spirit of selflessness, to help raise ethical and political awareness among the general public, and to foster a culture of civility across the country.

A robust institutional framework is key to enforcing ethical standards. It underpins and reinforces a long-term process of values education and promotion of ethical living. Guidelines for incorporating core socialist values into the effort to strengthen the rule of law were unveiled jointly by the General Offices of the CPC Central Committee and of the State Council (Two General Offices) in late 2016. Specific measures will be taken to integrate core socialist values into the process of strengthening the rule of law at the national level, into rule-based governance and into our social fabric to ensure that it informs each link of the legislative, law enforcement, judicial, and compliance processes and provides clear guidance for rewarding ethical behavior and punishing unethical acts.

RICH CULTURAL ACTIVITIES

An action plan for promoting fine traditions of culture -- the first of its kind -- was jointly issued by the Two General Offices on the eve of the Spring Festival -- the most important traditional holiday, adding another traditional touch to the festival. The move attracts widespread attention and adds to the momentum towards a cultural boom.

Cultural Industry Statistics, 2016

Category	Books	Radio shows	TV shows	TV animation	Films (drama)	TV series
Quantity	500,000	7.71 million hours	3.52 million hours	120,000 minutes	772	334

Cultural development has been in full swing in recent years, with artistic creations reaching a new peak. Cultural industries are thriving, and cultural infrastructure is being improved. The results are an increasingly diverse array of cultural options for the people, and growing cultural soft power and clout for the country. By the end of 2016, aggregate output of China's cultural industries reached 3.08 trillion yuan, equivalent to 4.14 percent of GDP. Currently, China leads the world in the number of TV series produced and books published, and is a close second in film production. Cultural development has not only translated into growing pride and confidence in the Chinese culture, but also enriches lives and gives people strength. Accompanying the people's growing aspirations for a better life are their demands for more

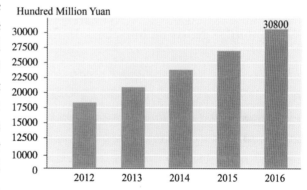

2012-2016 growth in cultural industries

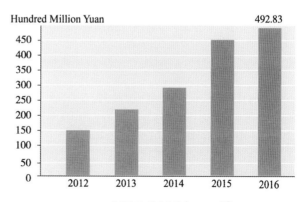

2012-2016 box office revenue

Wulanmuqi -- artists on horseback in the grasslands

Literally, wulanmuqi means "red tender shoots" in Mongolian; figuratively, it refers to "Revolutionary Artists on Horseback", a cultural task force that provides cultural and educational entertainment in a format uniquely suited to the sparsely populated grasslands. The first troupe of "Revolutionary Artists on Horseback" of Inner Mongolia had nine members and was founded in Sonid Right Banner, Xilingol League in 1957. The troupe's shows were very popular among local people. They were innovative, insightful, inspiring and fun. Many more such cultural task forces have since been established. Currently, the autonomous region boasts 74 active wulanmuqis, who put on more than 7,000 shows per year.

sophisticated cultural options. We must take the cultural industries to a new level in order to meet these demands.

A plethora of great art works and shows have come out -- great products that help quench the public's thirst for art, including *The Three-Body Problem, Thatched Memories, Nirvana in Fire, The Glory of Tang Dynasty, Monkey*

"The Beauty of Chinese Characters": Global Youth Design Contest

A global youth design contest entitled "the Beauty of Chinese Characters" was launched at the UNESCO headquarters in Paris in October 2015. It invited youths across the world to submit designs based on Chinese characters. As an occasion to encourage the exploration of the aesthetic value of ideograms, the event aimed to broaden global understanding and appreciation of the beauty of the Chinese script and to build a bridge of communication among youths of different cultural backgrounds. The first edition of the contest called for designs with a theme about the power of the heart, and received 1,250 submissions from 16 countries and regions. Outstanding submissions have been featured in itinerant exhibitions in various countries, including the United States and Japan. Pictured here is a group of winners and judges.

King: Hero Is Back, Operation Mekong, Chinese Poetry Competition, and *The Reader*, among others. Culture and the arts inspire a nation to move forward, and a brilliant future awaits our cultural industry. The key to promoting cultural development and prosperity is creating works of art that celebrate the national spirit and respond to today's challenges. Writers and artists should create insightful and well-crafted works that are grounded in the richness and diversity of everyday life and tell stories about our people.

Institutional reform propels cultural development. Significant progress has been made in this regard since the 18th CPC National Congress. An institutional framework has been in place, and over 300 reform measures unveiled. We must draw on our experience and lessons learned since then and speed up efforts in creating necessary mechanisms to ensure that cultural production delivers not only economic returns but also social benefits. Creative thinking and innovative measures are necessary to tackle pain points and unleash the potential of the cultural industries. Also important are measures to improve a public system of cultural service delivery to expand access to an increasing variety of cultural activities.

It is important to share our culture. Chinese culture belongs not only to the Chinese people but also to the world. China's growing prominence on the global stage leads to a growing need to tell our story and show the world a living and breathing China in all its dimensions. Efforts to share our culture should proceed within a larger framework of international cultural exchanges and cooperation. While we encourage borrowing from other cultures, we should do our best to preserve and promote our own traditional cultural treasures. It is crucial in this regard to enhance our communication capacity, in order to broaden our global reach and ensure clear and effective storytelling.

Culture is the linchpin between the past and the future. Our socialist culture with Chinese characteristics is grounded in our 5,000-year history, a history rich with heroic stories of strife, struggle and survival. It is one of the world's most vibrant and vigorous cultures, one that has a profound echo in our hearts, one that will thrive and shine in this new era.

Q&A

Q: What is meant by creative transformation and innovative development?

A: There is still some fine-tuning needed to make the quintessence of Chinese traditional culture compatible with a socialist market economy and the need for democratic governance. To promote our traditional cultural quintessence, it is necessary to strike a balance between continuity and change, to which creative transformation and innovative development are key. Creative transformation calls for modernizing what is valuable in our traditional culture and related forms of expression and breathing new life into them so as to reinvigorate their contemporary relevance. Innovative development, for its part, calls for enriching and refining our traditional cultural quintessence with elements of new social progress to broaden its reach and appeal.

Promoting Theoretical Awareness Is Essentially a Political Task

Cai Yongchun: At its core, promoting theoretical awareness is a political task; it requires us to take unequivocal positions, strengthen political consciousness, develop our ability to see a bigger picture, follow the directives of the central leadership, and align all our programs and initiatives with its agenda. It is important to reaffirm the authority and central leadership role of the CPC Central Committee with Xi Jinping at the center and attune our political thinking and actions to its guidelines. Also important are political skills in addition to political consciousness. We must hone our political acumen and judgment so that we will be in a better position to craft solutions.

CHAPTER 10

PUTTING THE PEOPLE FIRST

—Ensuring the wellbeing of the people and innovative social governance

Afilm entitled *Holding Hands,* released not long after National Day in October 2017, tells a story of how a rural village in Hunan, home to members of the Miao ethnic group, overcame heavy odds in its battle against poverty, thanks to the leadership of the CPC and the government. The film shows how unwavering perseverance, and targeted poverty reduction measures can be effectively implemented. It is many village-level efforts like this that can contribute to the global fight against poverty.

Since the 18th CPC National Congress in 2012, an area of special policy focus has been poverty reduction. The CPC has been committed from the start to creating a better life for the people. A number of new measures were unveiled at the recent 19th CPC National Congress to improve public well-being and to apply innovative ways to better social governance. The CPC is expected to always put the interests of the people first, and to promote social development so that the bounty of economic growth from reforms is more widely and fairly shared.

A PEOPLE-CENTERED APPROACH

A country thrives only when its people enjoy a good life. In his report to the 19th CPC National Congress, General Secretery Xi Jinping reiterated the founding aspirations and mission of the CPC to improve the lot of the Chinese people and bring about national renewal. The words "the people" appeared 203 times in the 30,000-word report, resonating strongly with the public and emphasizing that the CPC is steadfast and sincere in its people-centered approach to development.

The CPC is the people's party, with deep popular roots, and serving their interests. Party and people have gone through weal and woe together. They are inseparable like fish and water. This relationship is like boat and water, student and teacher, or servant and master. In the new era, commitment to our founding mission means focusing on working in the best interests of the people, and being ready and willing to respond to their concerns. Our achievements are measured by improvements in their wellbeing. Reform and development must rely on them, benefit them and improve their living standards.

For the people. In whose interests and for whom are the litmus tests for any political party or government. The CPC's founding mission is to serve the interests of the people. From the very beginning, the mission to liberate and bring happiness to our people has been engrained in our collective consciousness and has permeated all our revolutionary struggles, economic development drives and reform programs. That is why the CPC enjoys such popular support, and has been able to rally the nation to move forward. As we enter a new era, it is imperative that all Party members remain committed to this people-centered philosophy. Our actions must align with popular aspirations and wishes, and aim to create a better future for all.

Reliance on the people. Relying on the strength of the people is the key to success. History tells us that the people are the decisive force that drives societal development, and that they are the true creators of history -- the true heroes. The CPC has its roots among the people and always depends on their support. A review of history shows that whenever the CPC faced serious challenges, or whenever it arrived at a critical juncture for the nation's future, relying on the people helped it overcome the difficulties, and continue to move forward. In our march towards national renewal, it is critical to stay committed to this people-centered philosophy. Our strategies and initiatives are enriched and informed by input from the people and in turn they serve their needs. This reliance on the people builds cohesion and strengthens the momentum for making the Chinese dream come true.

Shared prosperity. As the creators of wealth, the people should rightfully share in it. This is a basic principle of socialism, and also the CPC's fundamental mission. The CPC's 19th National Congress recognized that the major challenge to address today is how to satisfy people's growing aspirations for a better life while our present development is still unbalanced and inadequate. This is raising new questions on how to share the fruits of growth. On the one hand, we must work hard to enlarge the economic "pie," on the other, make sure it is divided more fairly, so that everyone can benefit.

A SENSE OF SATISFACTION

Big things have small beginnings. Since 2015, a campaign to improve public restrooms has taken the nation by storm -- in popular tourist sites, urban districts, and rural areas. As of October 2017, 68,000 restrooms either newly built or renovated have appeared in tourist sites alone, winning praise from everyone by providing cleaner and more pleasant public spaces.

Establishing community service centers for senior citizens

Situated in the municipality of Chongqing, Yubei District has developed an innovative service approach in the past few years. A series of community senior service centers are being established to provide one-stop in-home services for the elderly, including nursing and medical check-ups. Entertainment and wellness activities are also organized. The photo shows senior citizens participating in a social event at one of the service centers.

Nothing is too small when it involves the public interest. Since 2012, improving the people's wellbeing has topped the Central Committee's agenda. Governing with a people-centered approach means priority is given to issues that bear most directly on the wellbeing of the populace, such as housing, education, healthcare, employment, elder care, and food safety. Many effective measures have been implemented to this end, making life more satisfying for our citizens.

This is an ongoing process that has no end. The guidelines proposed during the 19th CPC National Congress must be implemented to ensure people's wellbeing is improved, with shared accountability of all those responsible and with benefits to all the people. Our minimum goals must be met, and priority areas addressed. Institutional reforms must continue, and expectations properly managed. Within the limits of available resources, issues of special concern and anxiety must be dealt with one by one on a long-term basis, in particular as they relate to childcare, education, employment, healthcare, and housing.

Millions of families place their hopes for a better future on education. Better education for the people is paramount to national renewal. Thus we urgently need to modernize education. For this purpose, the CPC's educational guidelines must be implemented across the board. We must enhance ethical character-building and civic education and ensure equal access to education in rural and urban communities. Preschool instruction, special education, and online study are also areas of special focus. Efforts will continue to promote universal secondary schooling and improve vocational training. Also essential is the need to build world-class universities and academic programs. The financial aid system will be refined. Private schools will be supported, and appropriately regulated. Training is necessary to ensure the professional development of teachers. All of these measures aim at providing the younger generations with whole-person education that fosters moral, intellectual, and physical development, and prepares them to be builders in cause of socialism.

Employment is the biggest contributor to people's wellbeing. Its importance cannot be overemphasized. The CPC and the Chinese government have consistently pursued proactive employment policies that promote extensive job training, provide a full range of public services for job seekers, help break down institutional barriers to labor and talent flows, encourage the creation of high-quality jobs, and aim to achieve fuller employment.

Higher income is key to building a better life. The CPC and the government have been working to improve income distribution on the principle of worker output determining individual remuneration. Ensuring that income increases in step with economic and productivity growth is vital. Efforts will be made to expand the ranks of middle-income earners, increase the minimum wage, cap executive pay, and root out corruption and fraud, so as to narrow the income gap and ensure fairer distribution.

A safety net is indispensable. Currently, China has the world's widest national social security network, but issues of fairness and sustainability still persist. To address these challenges, the new CPC strategy calls for targeted measures to protect the most vulnerable, expand coverage and improve mechanisms to prevent anyone falling through the cracks. Efforts are on-going to build a sustainable, multi-tiered universal system of social security, covering urban and rural areas and providing adequate protection, with clearly defined responsibilities. On the issue of housing, curbing speculation is critical to ensuring that homes are affordable. Measures to alleviate shortages will include increasing supply from multiple sources, providing affordable housing through different channels, and expanding the home rental market.

Last but not least is healthcare. The health of its population is indicative of a nation's prosperity and provides the foundation for its citizens to experience both personal growth and a happy life. Implementing the Healthy China initiative requires more thorough reforms in the systems providing medical services, such as building a basic healthcare system suited to Chinese realities, providing universal health insurance and efficient high-quality care. Hospital management will be improved. National healthcare policies will be fine-tuned to ensure full, lifelong access.

THE FIGHT AGAINST POVERTY

In China, more than 60 million people have been lifted out of poverty since 2012 and the national poverty incidence has fallen below 4 percent. This is

131

Developing high-altitude vegetable gardening to overcome poverty

At the border of Guangxi and Guizhou, lies Tonglian Yao Ethnic Minority Village, situated in the chilly highlands of the Rongshui Miao Autonomous County, which is within the larger Guangxi Zhuang Autonomous Region. There is an ethnic minority population of 11,000 people and the county has a high poverty rate. In the last couple of years, China's targeted poverty alleviation policies helped the region take advantage of their geographic location to grow specialty crops, including high-altitude vegetables, sticky rice, and medicinal herbs. These measures helped local Yao people out of poverty. The photo shows an ethnic Yao girl picking mushrooms.

an amazing China Miracle that adds an impressive chapter to the history of mankind. As an international media outlet rightly put it: "China is a model for global poverty alleviation. Its experiences are significant contributions to world poverty reduction efforts."

The CPC and the Chinese government remain committed to eliminating rural poverty by 2020 based on current criteria.

We have now reached a crucial stage in the fight against poverty. A systematic push is needed to make breakthroughs in key areas. We must come together as a nation, and mobilize all resources possible to implement targeted measures. Anti-poverty efforts must include training and skills to empower those trapped in poverty so that they can help themselves. A three-pronged strategy will be pursued, combining specially targeted projects with sector-specific measures and whole-society involvement. Better effectiveness is key to winning the victory over poverty, and to eradicating extreme poverty for the first

Village in Tibet making great progress towards better livelihood

Nine families totaling 32 people live in a little Tibetan village called Yumai, nestled in the southern foothills of the Himalayas. Thanks to increasing support from the government, these families have been able to make a good living from family inns, tourism, transportation, woven goods, agriculture, and animal husbandry. In 2017, Yumai Village's annual income per capita exceeded 57,000 RMB, becoming a moderately well-off community. The image shows a villager tidying up a room in her family inn.

time in our nation's history. Such a victory will be of extraordinary significance not only for China but also for humankind.

There are still pockets of extreme poverty that defied previous alleviation attempts. In this final stage to root it out, creative thinking is needed to devise imaginative and directed strategies to overcome the most serious limitations and strenghten the weakest links.

Setting realistic goals, to ensure that, by 2020, rural residents still living in poverty, including those in extreme poverty, will meet their basic needs for food, clothing, compulsory education, basic healthcare, and housing. The next step will be to help these regions move closer to the national average. However, it would be unrealistic to expect places long afflicted by extreme poverty to reach parity with relatively developed regions by 2020. So we must be practical, set realistic goals, manage our expectations, and move forward one step at a time.

Pooling our resources will make it possible to implement large-scale alleviation projects. On a national level, the next step will be to focus on improving public services, infrastructure, and basic healthcare in areas of extreme poverty. Public instititutions and businesses in eastern regions and central government agencies are encouraged to participate and assist by providing funding, projects and personnel. As the saying goes, flames rise higher when everybody adds wood. Eradicating the last pockets of extreme poverty requires the input and contribution of all.

Accountability in implementation is essential. This requires proper deployment of personnel, clear division of responsibilities, and results-oriented strategies. Party committees and governments at all levels must place at the top of their agendas and take control of the struggle to eliminate the last pockets of extreme poverty. Coordination and integration are necessary to ensure that funds and personnel are deployed appropriately, projects are implemented effectively, and outcomes rigorously assessed. An annual poverty alleviation reporting and monitoring mechanism must be set up to ensure that anti-poverty measures proceed according to established timetables.

PUBLIC PARTICIPATION IN MAINTAINING SOCIAL ORDER

In recent years, volunteers from districts across Beijing, e.g., Chaoyang, Xicheng, Haidian, and Fengtai, have provided to the police important leads in the fight against illegal and criminal activities. They have become the eyes and ears of their communities, and have been effective in maintaining law and order in the nation's capital.

Safety is a basic human need. A secure environment is indispensable for

Public security volunteers on patrol in Beijing

economic and social development. It is important to strengthen civic governance in innovative ways to build lasting political and societal stability. The CPC's 19th National Congress called for building a participatory governance structure with effective mechanisms for conflict prevention and resolution. This will be guided by the Party and implemented by the government with the participation of civil society, the business community and the general public to ensure the rule of law and promote collaborative, rule-based, smart and effective governance.

The importance of public safety cannot be overestimated, since it bears directly on economic and social development, and the lives of millions of families across the nation. Workplace safety, as one instance, has improved with the total number of accidents decreasing for five years in a row. However, there have still been serious incidents resulting in major loss of life and property, with negative reverberations across society. It is imperative to stem the tide of major workplace incidents. A mentality of safety first must be a top priority, and a comprehensive system is needed for pooling resources and coordinating measures to prevent incidents, manage emergencies and determine responsibility. A workplace safety accountability system must be set up. In other aspects, society must also develop greater capability for disaster prevention, mitigation and response as part of ensuring harmony, safety and stability across the nation.

Law and order must be strengthened. It serves as a "barometer" for peace and stability. Since the 2012, integrated measures have led to improved law and order and greater public satisfaction. In 2012 the public gave an 87.55 percent approval rating to the security environment, and this increased to 91.99 percent in 2016. Our next step will be to build a nationwide 24/7 security video surveillance network that is well-coordinated and allows information sharing. In a coordinated approach, better Internet regulation and use of AI technologies will also be part of the effective public security network that protects personal security, property rights and dignity of individuals.

The overall social climate is also very important. Positive and forward thinking creates the correct environment for public harmony, order and contentment. Mainstream thinking in today's society is basically healthy and constructive, but there are negative and vulgar undercurrents, especially on social media. A combination of philosophical guidance, education and social counseling is needed to promote core socialist values, encourage moral and rational behavior, foster self esteem and confidence, and cultivate a general positive attitude to life.

Community governance is also vital, because local communities are where everyday life plays out. They are the bedrock of society. Past experience shows that the better the local public services the stronger the social cohesion and the greater the stability in a community. Giving greater authority to the community requires more participation by the local CPC organizations, local civil society groups, businesses and the residents in providing services and management. Coordinating all these actors will better address local concerns, enhance self-government and facilitate better government-public interactions.

A better life for the people is the fundamental objective of development. The CPC and the government are totally committed to this end. Past success comes from the people, and the future depends on them too. The interests, concerns and satisfaction of the people are the starting point for all our policies and efforts.

Q&A

Q: What is meant by world-class universities and academic programs?

A: In order to improve China's higher education and make it more competitive internationally, the central government has announced a major strategic plan to build world-class universities and academic programs. The aim is to encourage a group of top national universities and academic programs to become some of the world's best. A list of these universities and programs was unveiled in September 2017. The first group includes 137 institutions, of which, 42 universities will try to become the world's best (36 in Class A, 6 in Class B), and 95 universities with individual programs that have the potential of becoming the best. A total of 465 academic programs have been identified (44 selected by the universities themselves).

The need for a new participatory social governance structure

Pan Shengzhou (Head of the resident office of the Central Commission for Discipline Inspection at the Hong Kong and Macao Affairs Office of the State Council): China's new forms of industrialization, expanded use of IT, urbanization and agricultural modernization are all growing very rapidly. At the same time, profound economic transformations, realignments of interests, changes in ways of thinking and in social relations are also happening very fast. This rapidly evolving situation presents us with unprecedented challenges as we seek to ensure stable reforms and development, and defuse risks and tensions. We urgently need new thinking and innovation to create a stronger and better social governance structure that will ensure greater participation and involvement.

CHAPTER 11

BUILDING A BEAUTIFUL CHINA

—Making greater efforts to protect the environment

In its former days, Saihanba was the very definition of desolation, with nothing but lifeless sand as far as the eye could see. Today, however, the place is a verdant oasis, filled with greenery that stretches beyond the horizon. It took several generations to plan and build the Saihanba Forest in north China's province of Hebei, and the builders who created this miracle were given the Champions of the Earth award at the Third Session of the UN Environment Assembly held in December 2017, in Nairobi, Kenya. Saihanba's transformation from wasteland to forest is a vivid example of the saying that "green mountains and clean water are as precious as gold". It is an environmental success.

Environmental protection is a long-term endeavor: our hard work today will be rewarded only in the future. Improving the environment is included in the report to the 19th CPC National Congress as one of the goals for building a modern socialist country. The report outlines a roadmap for accelerating reform of the environmental protection mechanisms and building a beautiful China with blue skies, green landscapes, and clean waters.

PURSUING GREEN DEVELOPMENT: THE ONLY WAY FORWARD

Green is often called the color of life and nature. Green development is the only way to ensure harmony between man and nature. We must respect, adapt to, and protect the natural environment. Engaging in destructive practices is the same as shooting ourselves in the foot; ultimately, we are the ones who suffer. As early as over a century ago, Engels warned that people should not be intoxicated with their triumph against nature, as nature revenges on them for each of these triumphs. Since then, this warning has been borne out in countless environmental disasters.

The fate of civilization and that of the natural environment are intertwined. If one flourishes, both flourish; if one suffers, both suffer. Since the 18th National Congress, the CPC Central Committee led by Xi Jinping has displayed unparalleled political will and taken unprecedented measures to save the environment and fight pollution. Specific plans of action targeting air, water, and soil pollution have been implemented, effectively getting a number of major environmental problems under control. Major environmental protection and restoration projects have been on track. Envrironmental regulation has been strengthened. Our sustained efforts have led to steady improvement in environmental quality. We have pressed the "turbo mode" button for green development, placing our effort in the fast lane to build a beautiful China.

Meanwhile, we must acknowledge that China's environmental challenges remain daunting, and that improving our natural environment is a long-term process and an uphill battle. Modernization must be based on harmony between man and nature. Green development, therefore, should take center stage in our development drive, with a focus on energy and resource conservation, and environmental protection and restoration. Necessary conditions are called for in this connection, including rationalizing the spatial distribution of industries and patterns of production and consumption. Economic and social development and environmental protection must proceed in tandem.

It is important to move towards a green economy. Environmental problems are related to how the economy grows. Development and environmental protection must go hand in hand. Green development requires an enabling legal framework and related policy directives that facilitate the greening of production and consumption. An integrated approach should be pursued to promote a low-carbon circular economy, and transform a growth model that is excessively dependent upon economic expansion and resource consumption resulting in high emissions into a green growth model. We must tackle the problem at its source in order to achieve such a transformation and ensure complementarity between economic development and environmental protection.

We will encourage green innovation. Technology and financial support are

Residential photovoltaic systems benefting both the environment and local residents

In the last few years, Taixing, Jiangsu Province has made a big effort to promote residental photovoltaic systems. The city established fast-track approval procedures and provided one-stop solution for grid connection. Solar photovoltaic systems installed on rooftops can generate electricity for home use and surplus electricity can be sold to the national grid. Such systems help protect the environment and add to household income. Pictured here are national power grid workers maintaining a rooftop system.

indispensable for green development, which is propelled by green technology and green finance. Efforts in this regard include establishing a market-oriented system that encourages green innovation; promoting integration of scientific and technological innovation with environmental protection; developing green finance, including loans, insurance products, bonds, and mutual fund products that incorporate a green dimension; promoting the development and utilization of new materials, new energy, and new

Green economy in Zhangjiajie, Hunan offers promising prospect

In recent years, Zhangjiajie in Hunan Province has advocated the concept of green ecology and harmonious development. With equal emphasis on environmental protection and improvement of production and services, the city pursues a path of green, low-carbon and sustainable development. This photo shows a new-energy vehicle used to transport tourists to scenic sites.

---

technological processes; promoting energy conservation, clean production, and clean energy; and building an environmentally friendly economic structure.

Developing green energy remains an imperative. China's installed capacity for renewable energy is now at 24 percent of the global total, sealing China's place as the global leader in energy conservation and the utilization of new and renewable energy. We will continue the revolution in energy production and consumption, and accelerate the development of wind, solar, biomass, hydro, and geothermal energy. The development of safe and efficient nuclear energy will continue. We will redouble our efforts to promote resource conservation and recycling, reduce energy and resource consumption, improve energy efficiency, and build an energy system that is clean, low-carbon, safe, and efficient.

Green development entails concerted action across the society. It starts with each individual making small changes. It is critical to encourage moderation in resource use, promote green, low-carbon lifestyles, and combat extravagance, waste, and irrational consumption. Green practices should be promoted in all organizations, households, schools, and communities, and efforts will be on-going to green our travel. Every small step taken by an individual contributes to a giant leap towards building a beautiful China.

TACKLING THORNY ENVIRONMENTAL PROBLEMS

Twinkle, twinkle, little star…
Blue skies smiling at me; nothing but blue skies do I see.…

These are some of the most memorable lines from songs that depict natural beauty. While a common scene in the past, it is rarely seen today, in too many places. Pollution is taking its toll on the wellbeing of the people.

Improving environmental quality is a crucial dimension of our push to build a moderately prosperous society. Now and for the near-term, we must focus on resolving major environmental problems that impact public health. Environmental protection measures should be designed and implemented in the best interests of the people and in response to their concerns. These measures aim to prevent and control air, water, and soil pollution, and improve the quality of the environment and the wellbeing of the people.

One of the top priorities is reducing air pollution. Air quality in major cities has improved in comparison with the recent past, and this has not gone unnoticed as is evident from the public's enthusiastic reponse on social media. For 338 cities at the prefecture level or above, the average concentration of inhalable particles (PM10) in 2017 was 22.7 percent lower than in 2013. Likewise, comparing 2017 levels with 2013 levels, the average concentration

Multiple measures to tackle air pollution in Tianjin

In recent years, Tianjin has taken a number of measures to tackle atmospheric pollution, which include: substituting coal with natural gas or electricity; discontinuing coal-burning boilers, retrofitting them to burn other fuels, or replacing them with alternative-fuel boilers; taking tougher actions on polluting businesses; and tightening control on sources of fugitive dust pollution. These measures have been markedly successful.

According to statistics published on December 11, 2017 by the Ministry of Environmental Protection, Tianjin's average PM 2.5 concentration for November was 49 percent lower than the same period in 2016. This photo shows an EPA worker in Tianjin checking motor vehicles emissions.

of fine particles (PM2.5) was 39.6 percent lower in the Beijing-Tianjin-Hebei area; 34.3 percent lower in the Yangtze River Delta; and 27.7 percent lower in the Pearl River Delta. In Beijing itself, the concentration was 34.8 percent lower in 2017, reaching 58 mcg/m3. We need the efforts by the whole society to maintain the current momentum, tackling pollution at its source and making sustained efforts at air pollution control. It is also necessary to enhance coordination among major regions. These are things that must be done before there are more blue-sky days for people to enjoy.

Fighting water pollution is another priority. Water pollution directly affects people's daily life and health. In recent years, substantial progress has been made in water pollution control thanks to the implementation of a series of laws and policy initiatives, including the *Law on the*

"River chief and lake chief" systems to be implemented nationwide

In 2017, major progress was made in advancing the river management system nationwide. Plans were introduced on the provincial, municipal, county, and township levels, and 6 support systems were set up. A total of 310,000 people were designated as "river chiefs" at the township level, and 620,000 were made "river chiefs" at the village level, as part of a comprehensive system to be completed in 2018 for managing the country's rivers and lakes. Pictured here are a river chief and a professional public sanitation worker patrolling a local river in Changxing County, Zhejiang Province.

Prevention and Control of Water Pollution, Water Pollution Prevention and Control Action Plan, and *Decisions Concerning the Clean River Accountability System.* In 2017, the cross-sectional area ratio of good-quality water nationwide increased to 67.9 percent. Measures pursued under the stewardship of the CPC Central Committee include tightened water pollution prevention and control; integrated management of watershed and coastal areas; a systematic approach to the management of aquatic environments and water resources with restoration of aquatic ecosystems and the prevention and control of water-related disasters; dredging and cleaning up waterways, lakes and ponds where water quality is substandard and there is substantial contamination; and enhancing the protection of clean bodies of water and sources of drinking water to ensure the public's access to safe and clean drinking water and aquatic amenities.

Tackling soil pollution is also critical. An action plan for soil pollution prevention and control was unvailed in 2016, with emphasis on category-based and integrated measures, in particular, detailed surveys of soil pollution, strengthened enforcement of environmental rules and regulations, safe reutilization of polluted arable land, and the establishment of a national soil-environment monitoring network. In accordance with the guidelines outlined by the 19th CPC National Congress, the future focus will be on land used for agriculture and key industries and enterprises. Measures will be taken to survey the status of soil pollution, enhance soil pollution control and restoration efforts, strengthen the prevention and control of agricultural nonpoint source pollution, improve solid waste disposal and treatment systems, and step up rural habitat improvement campaigns to create a clean and pleasant living environment for the people.

ENHANCING ECOSYSTEM PROTECTION

All things in nature depend on each other and interact with each other, whether they are mountains, rivers, forests, streams, farm fields or grassy meadows. This means that any approach that focuses on one thing without regard to others will ultimately cause damage to the entire ecosystem. It is therefore essential to pursue a holistic approach to ecological protection that takes account of all variables spanning different areas and processes. Only such an approach can be effective in protecting our natural environment and ecosystems.

Ecosystems are the source of life and the wellspring of development. They cannot be replaced, and any serious damage to these systems will wreak havoc on our lives. Taking a holistic view of ecological protection, the 19th CPC National Congress emphasized the need to implement major projects for protecting and restoring key ecosystems, to strengthen ecological barriers, to build eco-corridors and biodiversity protection networks, and to improve ecosystem quality and stability. These are our long-term policies aimed at

Sanjiangyuan National Park to be officially established in 2020

The Sanjiangyuan region, located in the heart of the Tibetan Plateau, refers to the source area of three major rivers of Asia: the Yangtze River, the Yellow River, and the Lancang River which is also called Mekong after it flows beyond the Chinese boundary. In January 2018, the National Development and Reform Commission published the General Plan for the Sanjiangyuan National Park, which specified the official establishment of the Sanjiangyuan National Park in 2020. This is the country's first pilot park in the national park system.

preserving our environment and ecosystems and ensuring sustainable development.

Ecological-protection red lines are key to ecological security. These red lines must not be crossed, lest ecological security be put to risk. Institutional reforms are necessary to establish a nationally unified planning system for the use of land space, with coordinated efforts at the national, provincial (or regional or municipality) and further down to county levels, to draw the lines for land space control, i.e., land space to be used for ecological protection, farming, and urban development respectively, as a guide for development activities across the country.

Restoration is crucial. In the past five years, China has reclaimed more than 8 million hectares of desertified land, in a historic turnaround to reverse desertification. We will continue to take integrated measures to fight desertification, including rocky desertification, and soil erosion, enhance wetlands protection and restoration, and improve geological disaster prevention and control. Major projects will be implemented to protect natural forest resources, turn cultivated land back into forests, protect and restore wetlands, save and protect endangered and at-risk wildlife and flora, and create nature reserves. The fallow system will be applied on a more extensive scale to address degradation of cultivated land, grasslands, forests, rivers, and lakes, to allow a gradual recovery of the ecosystem.

Proper compensation is needed. It is necessary to set up a market-based, multifaceted compensation mechanism to compensate land owners for their lost income and opportunity due to ecological protection policies. It is also necessary to improve existing systems for the use of natural resources to make sure that users pay for what they use. Innovative market-based eco-compensation mechanisms will be explored to expand the scope of eco-compensation, and increase the use of transfer payments. A complete ban on development activities will be enforced in designated protected areas and key eco-function conservation zones. Protected areas and reserves that span provincial provincial boundaries will be established. Eco-compensation mechanisms will be put in place to address compensation issues for upstream and downstream areas of river basins.

REFORMING ENVIRONMENTAL REGULATION

It is an uphill battle to clean up the environment and more stringent measures are needed. There has been a big increase in the frequency and coverage of environmental inspections in recent years along with the rollout of an environemtal protection inspection program. Environemental inspection has become tougher and tougher. Since 2015, the central government has conducted environmental inspections covering all 31 provinces, autonomous regions, and municipalities, with more than 18,000 individuals subject to accountability review and more than 102,000 complaints addressed. An effective system of environmental accountability is now in place for local

CPC committees and government agencies. Such actions discouraged polluters and helped address a number of serious environmental concerns.

What has been achieved through environmental inspections reflects a positive change as a result of the environmental regulatory reform in recent years. The 19th CPC National Congress provided new guidelines on further reform in environmental regulation in order to rationalize the environmental protection and management system, so as to give more teeth to the regulatory process and increase its effectiveness.

Institution building is an important move in this connection. Environmental regulation requires a systematic approach that addresses issues in many aspects and that has to be done at the national level to ensure overall planning and effective leadership. The 19th CPC National Congress proposed the establishment of an agency at the national level for state-owned natural resources management and environmental protection oversight, as a central organization responsible for the management of all publicly owned natural resources, for the management of state-owned land resources and ecological restoration, and for monitoring pollution in all urban and rural areas and enforcing environmental rules and regulations. Designed to address the multifaceted nature of environmental regulation in a systematic manner, such a centralized institutional establishment helps resolve the problem of poor coordination among too many responsible agencies and too much buck-passing to get anything done.

Careful planning is indispensable. Environmental protection requires planning. Planning for public land use must be considered in an integrated manner by taking into account the purpose each subdivision serves, just like a house with different rooms for different purposes, bedroom, bathroom, kitchen, etc. A national land use and protection system will be established, with designated functions assigned to different regions, along with the corresponding fiscal, investment, business, land use, population, environmental, and performance review policies. Also underway is the plan to establish a natural reserve system built around national parks, a system with Chinese characteristics, aimed at creating an integrated structure for managing natural reserves, scenic areas, forest parks, and geological parks previously managed by different entities.

Rigorous enforcement is a must. Effective enforcement of environmental rules and regulations and harsh punishment for violations can serve as a deterence to would-be violators. Statistics shows that in 2016, nationwide, 137,800 alleged violations of environmental law were investigated, resulting in 124,700 guilty verdicts, and fines totaling 6.63 billion yuan, up 34 percent, 28 percent, and 56 percent respectively. The number of cases investigated and the amount of fines imposed were both unprecedented. Effective deterrence and stringent enforcement must continue, together with heavy fines and harsh punishments, to stop any act that harms the environment, foster a culture that deters and discourages environmentally unfriendly practices, and reverse a weak environmental protection trajectory.

Environmental protection entails sustained efforts. It concerns not only the present generation, but also generations to come. It is essential for sustainable development. Xi Jinping Thought on Socialism with Chinese Characteristics for a New Era and the principles outlined by the 19th CPC National Congress are of immediate relevance to the country, as they provide the guidance for green development, and call for sustained efforts for generations to preserve and protect our natural environment. We will continue our development in a way that ensures harmony between man and nature and work together to build a beautiful China.

Seeking harmony between man and nature and satisfying people's demand for a beautiful environment

Li Ganjie (Minister and Secretary of CPC Leadership Group, Ministry of Environmental Protection)

There have been profound changes in the public's demands. In the past, what people needed was adequate food and clothing, and the concerns were about survival. Now, people are concerned about the ecology and environment. As people puruse better lives, they want to live in a beautiful environment. Providing more high-quality ecological products has therefore become a new challenge in the new era. We must bring peace and beauty back to nature and maintain harmony between man and nature before we can satisfy people's desire for a beautiful environment.

CHAPTER 12

BUILDING A BETTER AND HARMONIOUS WORLD

—Creating a community of shared future

We live in a world of many different countries and civilizations. Just as a single flower does not create the beauty and splendor of an entire garden in spring, the efforts of all countries are needed to make the world a better place. Countries and civilizations, different as they are, all have their individual strengths and must work together for collective development in order to build a more beautiful world for humanity.

We live in a world of diversity and great changes. It is important that countries make their best efforts to seek common ground despite differences and ensure that competition produces win-win outcomes. Resolved to make its contribution to a better world, China has put forward the important concept of building a global community of shared future.

A WORLD GOING THROUGH PROFOUND CHANGES

In complicated situations, we must see the big picture before we can take the initiative. In today's rapidly changing world, China must keep abreast with global trends and keep the best interests of humanity in mind as it takes up its responsibility as a major power and helps create a promising future for the world.

"It was the best of times, it was the worst of times." Charles Dickens' words are as true today as they were 160 years ago, when he wrote about the period after the Industrial Revolution. Today, we are living in a world with similar paradoxical situations. As the world undergoes tremendous developments and changes, we bathe in the sunshine of peace while still facing the danger of war. We enjoy the fruits of development and progress, but still cannot eliminate the root causes of poverty and backwardness. We share the benefits of cooperation, but suspicion among countries lingers on. Many people are confused and wonder what has become of this world we live in.

This is a world of peaceful development. Peace and development are still the hallmarks of the times and the prevailing trends of today. Having gone through centuries of countless wars, in which millions lost their lives and homes, mankind detests war and dearly cherishes hard-earned peace. People have never been so enthusiastic in their aversion to war. In today's world, the forces of peace overpower the threats of war. Indeed, people support peace deep in their hearts. Development, prosperity, fairness, and justice have become the norm, and dialogue and peaceful negotiations are used in place of confrontation as effective approaches for settling disputes among countries.

This is a world full of hope. Changes are taking place each and every day in today's world. Development and progress have brought an increasing number of positive elements to the world: multi-polarity in world politics, advances in economic globalization, and unprecedented levels of exchange of ideas and cultures, pushing human civilization to the highest level of development in history. Information technology, in particular, has experienced exponential growth, bringing about new technologies and inventions in ways that have profoundly changed the way we work and live. We are more confident and determined than ever before to overcome difficulties and create a better future.

This is a world of constant change. Changes in the global governance system and the international order stem from changes in the balance of power in the world. The 21st century witnessed the rise of emerging economies and developing countries, represented by China, and those countries collectively contribute 80 percent of global economic growth. The result has been the most dramatic change in the balance of power in modern times. Against this backdrop, emerging economies have been increasingly involved in developing a new international economic and political order, leading to an accelerated pace in the evolution and reconstruction of the global governance system.

This is a world of ceaseless challenges. Life on earth is not always bathed in sunshine, rather it is often shrouded in dark clouds. Challenges such as conflicts, power politics, financial crisis, gaps in development, terrorist attacks, the refugee crisis, and others are presenting themselves all the time. Crises like the "gray rhino" and "black swan", in particular, were dangers that are difficult to prevent. These are daunting challenges in today's world that endanger people's lives and pose a serious threat to peaceful development.

People may wonder what kind of a world this is after all. As a matter of fact, we live in a world of uncertainties, dealing with both the bright and dark sides of it: hope and disappointment, opportunities and challenges. We should not give up on our dreams merely because the reality around us is too complicated. We should not stop pursuing our ideals because they seem to be out of reach. The future of the world is in the hands of the people of all countries, and the future of mankind hinges on the choices it makes. The Chinese people are ready to work together with people of all countries in a joint effort to build a community of shared future and create a bright future for mankind.

THE CHINESE PROPOSITION FOR A HARMONIOUS WORLD

General Secretary Xi Jinping elaborated on the idea of a community of shared future in many important settings: the Moscow Institute of International Relations, United Nations Office in Geneva, the Boao Forum for Asia, the Davos Forum, the G-20 Summit in Beijing, and the high-level dialogue between the CPC and leaders of political parties from other countries. On each of these occasions, he delivered a clear message to the world: people of all countries live in the same global village, and with increased interdependence, we are all part of a community of shared future.

So, what kind of a community is it? In a nutshell, it is a community with "five dimensions", namely politics, security, economy, culture, and ecology. In General Secretary Xi Jinping's vision for the community of a shared future, we need to make major progress in these five areas in order to build a world that has lasting peace, universal security, common prosperity, openness and inclusiveness, and a clean and beautiful environment.

Lasting peace is the cornerstone. Peace is like air and sunlight in that we cannot live without it. Without a peaceful environment, building a community of shared future becomes nothing more than an elusive goal. It is the simple wish of the people of the world to live in peace, not war. Countries must respect each other and consult with each other on an equal footing. There must be a new type of state-to-state relationship that is based on dialogue instead of confrontation, partnerships instead of alliances. We must be free from the Cold War mentality and power politics. Only when that happens can the peoples of the world live in harmony and pursue development in a peaceful, stable, and beautiful world.

Universal security should serve as a safety net. Safety is the top priority for humanity. Traditional and non-traditional security threats alike have been increasing, posing risks to people of different ethnic groups, countries, and regions. No place on earth is unaffected and no country can isolate itself from these risks. Countries must work together to pursue common, comprehensive, cooperative, and sustainable security to form a global safety net in order to keep people away from danger and fear.

Shared prosperity is the fundamental goal. An important phenomenon of the world economy today is the global flow of goods, capital, information, and talent, which has resulted in an irreversible trend of economic globalization. A world in which everyone is better off is the true definition of our success. Countries must work together to build an open world economy so that they may collectively have the capabilities to tackle financial crises, economic recessions, and market risks. They can all be part of economic globalization and share the benefits of economic growth.

Development should be characterized by openness and inclusiveness. Planet earth is home to more than 7 billion people in more than 200 countries and regions. They belong to more than 2,500 ethnic groups, speak more than 5,000 languages, and follow many different religions. Human civilization consists of many different societies and each exists as a result of the collective wisdom and hard work of a specific nation or ethnic group. No civilization is higher or lower than any other, and none is superior or inferior to the others. Each has its own strengths and they all coexist. As they learn from each other in peaceful coexistence, filling in knowledge gaps by drawing on the experiences of others, human civilization as a whole will flourish and thrive.

A clean environment is the foundation. The earth is our only home, and it must be cherished and protected. While industrial development has created unprecedented material wealth over the previous few centuries, it has caused irreparable ecological trauma. Global warming, ozone layer depletion, drastic declines in biodiversity, and atmospheric pollution are signs of a deteriorating environment which threatens human survival. In order to achieve harmony between man and nature on a path of sustainable development, countries must respect and protect the environment and build up a global ecological system for green, sustainable development.

INTERNATIONAL COOPERATION UNDER THE BELT AND ROAD INITIATIVE

In May 2017, 29 national leaders along with more than 1,600 representatives from 140 countries and 80 international organizations arrived in Beijing for the Belt and Road Forum for International Cooperation. It was an impressive event, with an unprecedented level of participation, successful outcomes for cooperation in the spirit of the Silk Road, and splendid theatrical performances, leaving a deep impression on the participants and the world.

The success of the Belt and Road Forum demonstrated that China has the rallying power and ability to launch initiatives of great influence. It also was a conference that showcased the achievements in the Belt and Road Initiative. Over the past four years, the initiative has turned from concept to action, from vision to reality, as it garners support from an increasing number of countries. More than 80 countries and international organizations have signed cooperation agreements with China, indicating that China's "circle of friends" continues to expand. Substantive progress has been made under the initiative, with the Asian Infrastructure Investment Bank and the Silk Road Fund up and running, a large number of landmark basic projects in the implementation phase, and people-to-people exchanges underway in various areas. These developments have proven that the Belt and Road Initiative is in the interests of the countries it encompasses, and the project is one that leads to peace, prosperity, openness, innovation, and progress in civilization.

The Belt and Road Initiative has now reached an important stage where greater efforts are needed to accelerate the implementation and improve quality through detailed planning and solid work. As foreign investment

The Golden Bridge, on display at the site of the Belt and Road Forum for International Cooperation, is a symbol of communication and peaceful development for the benefit of all the countries along the route.

comes in, Chinese companies are also engaging abroad. Projects should be developed and implemented through consultation and collaboration to achieve shared growth. Capacities for innovation and openness should be increased in a new phase of all-around, bidirectional opening up, with links running eastward and westward over both land and sea. Efforts under the initiative should be further aligned with the development strategies of the countries along the route in order to achieve policy coordination, connectivity of infrastructure and facilities, unimpeded trade, financial integration, and closer people-to-people ties. The initiative will serve as a new platform for international cooperation, providing a fresh impetus for development among various countries.

Focused efforts are needed. The Belt and Road Initiative is an enormous

China-Europe railway links bringing opportunities to countries along the Silk Road

Since March 19, 2011 when the first train left for Europe under a direct international goods transport program between China and Europe as well as other countries along the Belt and Road route, more than 6,000 trips have been made, running on 57 routes, connecting 35 Chinese cities with 34 cities in 12 European countries. Pictured here is the opening ceremony of the China-Europe Express.

project that needs focused efforts in key areas. Scattered efforts here and there across a broad expanse simply will not do. It is necessary to remove bottlenecks by focusing on significant routes, cities, and projects. We will start with a number of important projects in key areas such as infrastructure interoperability, integrated development and utilization of energy resources, transnational trade and economic cooperation zones, and joint R&D in core technologies. Results from these projects can subsequently be replicated in other areas.

Supporting policies must be in place. For the Belt and Road Initiative to move forward, it is important to ensure connectivity among the countries in policy, infrastructure, trade, and finance, and there must be increased people-to-people exchanges. As we design the policies, we must make sure that they are aligned with the development plans of the relevant countries and regions, so that policies are consistent, and a favorable policy environment is created for the implementation of the initiative. Financing is the lifeline of the initiative. The Asian Infrastructure Investment Bank and the Silk Road Fund, therefore, must fulfill their roles as important sources of funding, and cooperation should be increased among financial institutions and financial markets to build a support system providing ample financing for the implementation of the Belt and Road Initiative.

Efforts from all sectors are needed. As the saying goes, many hands make light work. The Belt and Road Initiative is an ambitious undertaking that requires support from the government and the market in a joint effort in order for it to be a success. Aside from the leading role played by the government, it is also important for businesses, non-governmental organizations, think tanks, and the media to be involved. Essentially, it is an endeavor led by the government, with the participation of businesses and further support from the public.

The Belt and Road Initiative is somewhat like a ribbon in that it keeps pearls along the road strung together. Though initiated by China, it is not a solo performance by China. It is a chorus to be sung by all countries involved. Only when each and every country is fully motivated to work towards our common interests will the Belt and Road Initiative become a truly grand symphony of shared future, bringing harmony and benefit to everyone.

DIPLOMACY WITH CHINESE CHARACTERISTICS

Since the 18th CPC National Congress in late 2012, General Secretary Xi Jinping has traveled almost 200 days, visiting over 60 countries and major international and regional organizations on more than 30 international trips covering 600,000 kilometers. His diplomatic activities have made friends

The CPC in dialogue with world political parties

From December 1 to 3, 2017, the Communist Party of China convened a high-level dialogue with political parties from other countries, with the theme: "Working together towards a community with a shared future for mankind and a better world: responsibility of political parties". Held in Beijing, the nation's capital, the conference was attended by leaders of over 300 political parties or organizations from more than 120 countries. This was the first international event organized in China after the 19th CPC National Congress. It was the first time that the CPC held a high-level dialogue with various political parties around the world on such a large scale. Pictured here are some of the political party leaders attending the dialogue.

and partners for China and brought the country to center stage globally to an extent that has never been seen before.

Over the last five years, important progress has been made in China's diplomacy. Past, present, and future, the country adheres to the principles of peace, development, cooperation, and shared benefit for the purpose of

Providing medical assistance to developing countries

In 1963, China was invited to dispatch a medical team to North Africa, and since then, China has provided medical assistance to 66 countries and regions in Asia, Africa, Latin America, Europe and Oceania. As of 2013, 24,000 medical staff had served on these teams, and treated 270 million patients. Medical assistance is an important part of China's foreign aid, and has been welcomed by people in these countries. It embodies the responsibility that China takes upon itself as one of the major countries in the world. Pictured here are doctors from a Chinese medical team performing a screening test for children's congenital heart disease in Afghanistan.

safeguarding world peace and promoting common development. China has been engaged in friendly cooperation with other countries on the basis of the five principles of peaceful coexistence and pushed for a new type of international relations based on mutual respect, fairness and justice, and cooperation for win-win outcomes. As one of the world's major countries, China has been advancing its diplomacy with dignity and confidence.

Diplomatic activities and links should be increased. Over the past five years, China's diplomacy has covered much of the world, from General Secretary Xi Jinping's first visit to Russia as Chinese President to his meeting with US President Trump in the Forbidden City in Beijing; from the Shanghai summit of the Conference on Interaction and Confidence Building in Asia to the APEC meeting in Da Nang, Vietnam; from the Johannesburg Forum on China-Africa Cooperation to the high-level dialogue between the CPC and political parties from other countries. China has made major headway in its relations with other countries, building partnerships with major countries, neighboring countries, and developing countries alike. Such efforts will intensify as China continues to develop relations of friendship and cooperation with all countries: maintaining sound relationships with the United States, Russia, EU countries, and the BRICS countries, pursuing its neighborhood diplomacy with countries in Northeast, Southeast, and Central Asia, and enhancing its relations and cooperation with developing countries. With such a comprehensive and multilevel approach, China is well-positioned in international affairs as it works for a new type of international relations based on mutual respect, fairness and justice, and cooperation towards win-win outcomes.

Reform of the global governance system should be promoted. General Secretary Xi Jinping has emphasized that global governance is inadequate. Such an imbalance, often referred to as a "deficit in global governance", is a tough issue to address and the international community expects to hear China's voice and ideas. China will continue to be an active part of reforming that system, promoting and leading the process. China believes that the world needs a governance system that is based on the principles of consultation, joint contribution, and shared benefit, and that international relations should become more democratized. All countries – large and small, strong and weak, rich and poor – must be equal participants in global governance. The representation and voice of developing countries should be expanded in the arena of international affairs, and a push should be made for a fairer and more just global governance system.

China is taking up its responsibilities as a major country. A Chinese saying tells us to "always keep in mind the interests of the entire world". This is what China said and it is what it has done. As its profile in the international arena grows, China has done a great deal to defend the authority and status of the United Nations and has taken on more responsibilities and obligations. China has been an active and generous participant in international affairs in the context of peacekeeping, disaster relief, the response to climate change, combating terrorism, and nuclear non-proliferation. As China becomes stronger it will do even more within its capabilities, and will make greater contributions to global peace and development.

Since ancient times, people have always dreamed of a better life, wherever they live. The community of shared future is a beautiful vision and promise that China has presented to the world, but it will not automatically manifest itself. It will require the peoples of the world to sustain their efforts in order to make it a reality. China will join hands with all countries in the world, so that together we can create a better home for humanity on planet earth.

The idea of a community of shared future: an important creation in China's diplomacy

Wang Yi (Minister of Foreign Affairs)

The concept of a global community of shared future is rooted in thousands of years of Chinese civilization and the vast experiences of China's diplomatic activities. It meets the desires of countries for peace, development, cooperation, and progress. It emphasizes the need to establish partnerships in which all countries are equals and their relations are based on mutual understanding and consultation; to create a security structure that is based on fairness, justice, joint contributions and shared benefits; to increase communication among civilizations to promote harmony, inclusiveness and respect for differences; and build an ecosystem that puts Mother Nature and green development first. These five goals constitute the community of shared future for humanity, as an important creation in China's diplomacy with Chinese characteristics.

BUILDING A PARTY THAT DOES NOT FAIL

—Enforcing strict Party discipline

Shortly after the conclusion of the 19th CPC National Congress, the newly constituted Political Bureau of the CPC Central Committee convened its first meeting on October 27, 2017. It considered and adopted a set of detailed criteria for tightened implementation of the Eight Rules issued in December 2012, including spending limits for activities such as research and investigations, conferences, briefings and official visits. This represents a call to action for ethical conduct. As an "upgraded version" of the Eight Rules, the new rules are a powerful weapon in the fight against unethical conduct, thus dispelling the misconception that it is time to relax Party discipline, and reaffirming the CPC's commitment and determination to strict internal management.

A new era means new expectations. Just as it takes a good blacksmith to make good products, our Party must stay true to its promise to set an example in enforcing ethical standards. As we position ourselves at a new starting point in our effort to pursue socialism with Chinese characteristics and realize our dream of national renewal, we must continue to build the Party by making it stronger through better discipline and renewed committment, so that it remains a dynamic governing Marxist party at the forefront of the times, enjoying popular support, able to carry out self-revolution, and to withstand all tests.

ENFORCING PARTY DISCIPLINE: AN UNENDING PROCESS

The public's satisfaction has been growing with the CPC's ethics enforcement, as shown by figures released by the National Bureau of Statistics: 81 percent in 2013; 88.4 percent in 2014; 91.5 percent in 2015; and 92.9 percent in 2016. These numbers reveal widespread public approval for achievements in enforcing Party discipline over the past few years. They also show strong public support for and confidence in the CPC's ability to renew itself.

Hunting down overseas fugitives and recovering stolen funds

Since the 18th CPC National Congress, an anti-corruption operation "Skynet" has been launched and a number of fugitives hiding overseas have been brought to justice. As of December 6, 2017, 51 of China's 100 most wanted corruption suspects on Interpol's "Red Notice" list had been brought back. In 2017 alone, a total of 1,021 non-listed fugitives have been returned, including 292 Party members and public officials, and 903 million yuan was recovered. Pictured here is Xu Xuewei, one of the suspects on the most-wanted list.

A political party must hold a high standard of integrity. Since the CPC's 18th National Congress, the Central Committee under the stewardship of Xi Jinping has been making unprecedented efforts to promote integrity and fight corruption. This is an uphill battle that requires courage and determination: courage to go beyond the superficial to root out deep-seated corruption, and determination to live up to the expectations of 1.3 billion people in spite of heavy odds. The campaign aims to tackle, first and foremost, issues that are the most loathed and that threaten the legitimacy of the CPC as the ruling party. We are firmly resolved to implement the Eight Rules, enforce discipline and regulations through inspections that are effective deterrents to graft, and root out corruption. Substantial progress has been made, bringing a breath of fresh air to the Party and the government, and boosting morale among Party members and the public.

Especially encouraging is the fact that the "Chinese formula" has proved effective in fighting corruption, which is a persistent worldwide scourge. The hunt for "tigers" (corrupt senior officials), "flies" (corrupt low-ranking bureaucrats) and "foxes" (fugitives abroad suspected of major economic crimes) has been moving full steam ahead, leading to the elimination of these malignant tumors one by one and creating an unstoppable momentum.

Deterrence goals have basically been met. Statistics show that over the past five years since the 18th CPC National Congress, national disciplinary and oversight agencies have received 2.67 million complaints, investigated 1.54 million cases, disciplined 1.53 million officials, and 58,000 cases were brought under criminal proceedings. Among those investigated, 440 were high-ranking officials, including some at or above the provincial level. Among the "100 most-wanted" suspects of fraud hiding overseas, for whom red notices were issued by Interpol, 51 have been brought back. The unprecedented scale and severity of the crackdown on corruption over the past five years show the resolve of the CPC to maintain momentum to ensure a zero-tolerance policy with no corner out of bounds and no stone left unturned. The crackdown will target, in particular, those officials still in important positions and even on track to be promoted but who nonetheless since the 18th CPC National Congress have not changed their unethical conduct and thus aroused strong popular reactions. These stringent measures will serve as powerful deterrents and send a stern warning to all officials against the peril of corruption.

Building a strong institutional framework is the most potent antidote against corruption. Effective institutional controls are a long-term, fundamental solution to blocking loopholes. Since 2012, the CPC has developed and revised over 90 sets of internal rules and regulations. These include the Eight Rules, the revised CPC Disciplinary Inspection Regulations, the revised CPC

Disciplinary Action Regulations, the CPC Accountability Regulations, the CPC Intra-Party Supervision Regulations, and the CPC Transparency Regulations (Provisional). The implementation of these rules and regulations will tighten and strengthen institutional controls.

Strong beliefs and character building are the best defenses against corruption. Confessions of those found guilty of fraud show that a lack of both opens the door to wrongdoing. It is therefore critical to protect the bottom line of moral and ethical behavior. Since 2012, a series of educational initiatives have been launched within the CPC, to review discipline enforcement, with necessary input from the public, and to apply higher standards of self-cultivation, self-discipline, and integrity. These activities also include workshops and study sessions on how to implement the CPC's constitution and rules and instructions from the central leadership, and how to become a worthy Party member. Through these activities, CPC members and officials have had a better understanding of Xi Jinping Thought on Socialism with Chinese Characteristics for a New Era, and deepened their sense of what the Party stands for with greater conviction of the mission and goals of the CPC.

Progress over the past five years has won high praise from the people, but it is not time to pause. The recent 19th CPC National Congress reaffirmed the need to continuously enforce strict Party discipline. In accordance with the Party-building guidelines for the new era, this process will go on with a special focus on systematic, rigorous and effective measures to make the CPC stronger.

OVERALL GUIDELINES FOR PARTY BUILDING IN A NEW ERA

The guidelines unveiled at the 19th CPC National Congress offer a wide perspective, outlining an ambitious and detailed plan for building the Party in the new era.

This plan provides basic direction. It urges that Party building follows two established principles: ensuring and strengthening the leadership role of the CPC; and ensuring effective intra-Party supervision and discipline. The outcomes of all efforts will also be measured against these principles. The first principle reaffirms the CPC's leadership in all aspects of life across the land, including government, national defense, economic and social development, in addition to Party affairs. Strong Party leadership is vital because it is the anchor of China's form of socialism. This is the starting point for all Party building efforts in the new era. The second principle emphasizes the need for effective intra-Party supervision and discipline enforcement, because they are essential to protecting the progressive nature and integrity of the Party and ensuring public support. They are therefore key to the survival of the CPC and the future of our nation.

The plan identifies four substantive areas to focus on: (a) long-term capacity building for governance, and to protect the progressive nature and integrity of the CPC; (b) strong political integrity; (c) firm ideals, convictions and a sense of purpose; and (d) mobilizing initiative, creativity and innovation. These form the substance of Party building in the new context.

The plan outlines specific strategies. These include increasing a sense of political identity and philosophical conviction, improving organizational arrangements, promoting ethical conduct, discipline enforcement and institution building to counter corruption and wrongdoing. This is a new approach to combining theory with practice: incorporating both a stronger sense of political identity and discipline into the Party building framework highlights the primary importance of both for tackling the root causes of today's ills. This new approach reflects the CPC's understanding of its governance imperatives, and the need for a rigorous, systematic approach to Party building in the new context.

The plan lays out our primary goal, which is to build a dynamic Marxist party that is at the forefront of the times, enjoys popular support, has the courage to remake itself, and is able to overcome challenges. Each of these elements is of great significance, and together, they summarize the nature of the CPC, its purpose and mission, its values, political disposition, as well as its fundamental aspiration to work for the wellbeing of the people and the national rejuvenation.

THE IMPORTANCE OF POLITICAL INTEGRITY

One of the important innovations that emerged at the 19th CPC National Congress was to highlight the importance of politicial integrity and awareness as part of Party building. This has great significance for the Marxist theory of Party building.

A political party is by definition political in nature, so a strong sense of political integrity and awareness within it is only natural. Our own experience in Party building shows that such elements are the only way of ensuring we follow the right direction, remain steadfast in our principles, and achieve unity and cohesion within the Party.

Strong political awareness has always been a requirement for Party members. When they have the political awareness, there will be healthy political activities within the Party, and then the organization is united and vigorous, and Party work moves forward. In the opposite case, when people are divided and demoralized, and wrong ideas are not addressed promptly, serious problems surface that damage the work of the Party. History and current realities all demonstrate time and again that adherence to Party principles and regulations has a direct bearing on its future and whether or not its cause is successful.

Since 2012, the Central Committee has taken a series of important measures to build a stronger sense of political awareness and identity, tighten Party leadership, regulate internal Party political activities, step up supervision and education, enforce ethical standards, and push forward the anti-graft campaign. Substantial progress has been achieved, leading to stronger centralized leadership, profound changes within the Party itself, and a substantially improved image to the public.

Strengthening political integrity and awareness is central to Party building. It is core to the guidelines of the 19th CPC National Congress, and therefore of fundamental importance. It determines the direction and effectiveness of all efforts. It underpins all the other aspects of Party building, which include political philosophy, organization, ethical conduct, and discipline. A stronger political awareness will lay the groundwork for progress in all related areas. Implementing these guidelines means taking an unequivocal political stand, strictly adhering to Party rules and regulations, and consciously applying Party principles to all actions.

The fundamental objective of this focus on political awareness is to build unity and cohesion within the CPC. It means we are clear about our political stand. This means affirming General Secretary Xi Jinping's prime position within both the Central Committee and the Party, and supporting the authority and central leadership of the Central Committee. All thinking and actions must be fully aligned with the Central Committee. We must follow the Party constitution, which means properly regulating political activity within the Party, applying the rules of democratic centralism, promoting and commending the values of integrity and loyalty, fairness and decency, respect for truth, and clean governance. Duplicity and double-dealing are totally unacceptable. When all Party members have fulfilled these requirements and are able to examine and assess events and situations from a clear political standpoint, to plan appropriately and take suitable actions, the unity of the Party will be assured and it will be able to lead and coordinate all sectors of society.

Party officials at all levels, and high-ranking ones in particular, must first and foremost have built up the necessary political awareness. The more matters they have to deal with, the more risks and difficulties they face, the more important this becomes. They must pay greater attention to following Party principles, sharpening political sensitivities, and improving political skills. All CPC members must be loyal to the Party, be willing to share the Party's concerns and responsibilities, and work for the best interests of the people.

PARTY ETHICS AND THE FIGHT AGAINST CORRUPTION

From January 11 to 13, 2018, the CPC Central Commission for Discipline Inspection convened its second meeting in Beijing. General Secretary Xi Jinping emphasized the importance of CPC leadership in the new era of socialism with Chinese characteristics and consequently the need for new thinking and action in response to new realities. We must implement the outcomes of the 19th CPC National Congress and make a new start with renewed efforts to enforce Party discipline, in a new chapter of Party building.

Promoting integrity and fighting corruption is like rowing upstream: not to advance means being washed backwards. Building a clean Party is a long and complex process, and we must understand that the protracted struggle requires determination, tenacity and courage in the face of many odds.

The Party's code of conduct must be enforced. General Secretary Xi Jinping issued instructions in December 2017 on the need to relentlessly fight deep-seated and undesirable conduct and tendencies, in particular, form over substance, red tape, self-indulgence, and wastefulness. These are recurring issues and need to be continuously corrected. Leaders at all levels must set the example, nip any sign in the bud no matter how trivial it is, take strong action to prevent them from spreading, and build on the present results of the Eight Rules. All Party members must follow the CPC's discipline requirements, and make the implementation a life habit, like a second nature.

Discipline must be strengthened. Respect for laws and regulations, and effective enforcement bring stability across the land. The Party must organize regular compliance training and cite examples of good and bad discipline as both encouragement and warning. Strict self-discipline should become instinctive and customary for all Party members and officials. Criticism and self-criticism should be employed for identifying and addressing problems. A "Four-level" scale is in use for oversight and discipline: 1) oral warning, 2) written censure, 3) demotion, 4) criminal investigation. This must be applied in a timely way to stop an emerging problem from becoming serious. In the pipeline are more refined rules and regulations in relation to ethical issues, monitoring of official conduct, and oversight to create a stronger institutional framework.

Our fight against corruption is unrelenting. There is nothing more hated by the public than corruption. It is also the most serious threat to the CPC. This continues to be a complex and extremely fierce struggle. At this point we have the upper hand and our resolve to prevail is unwavering. This is a zero-tolerance crackdown that will leave no corner out of bounds and no stone left unturned. In cases of bribery, both the giver and taker will be severely punished. Measures will be taken to reduce case backlogs. A special focus will be on catching transgressions early, trapping both "tigers" and "flies" as soon as they emerge. To tackle both symptoms and root causes, we need stronger anti-corruption legislation and better mechanisms to report alleged violations. A discipline inspection system will be put in place at the county and city Party committee level so as to deal with grassroots corruption. No matter where they are, the corrupt will be caught and brought to justice.

An integrated oversight system is indispensable. A fragmented approach will be ineffective. We must build and refine an integrated system that will cover the whole Party and the entire country. It will be led by the Party, with broad authority, and the power to deal with problems at all levels and in all aspects of public life, and to enforce accountability of all public servants. The anti-corruption "Skynet" will be tightened, a top-down and bottom-up approach to oversight as well as peer oversight will provide full coverage without blind spots. The work of Party officials will be monitored to ensure that the authority granted them by both Party and public is not abused, and that abusers are swiftly punished. A more effective circuit of on-site political inspections will provide fast, bottom-up channels to identify and address problems and serve as effective deterrents.

BUILDING CAPACITY FOR GOVERNANCE AND LEADERSHIP

The leadership of the CPC is the defining feature of socialism with Chinese characteristics, and represents the greatest advantage of our distinct socialist system. China is a country led by the CPC. If socialism with Chinese characteristics is compared to a gigantic ship, the CPC is its helmsman. This ship is now crossing turbulent waters and has to brave billowing waves and steer clear of hidden reefs. This is a critical juncture so the helmsman's skills are paramount. That is why we must strengthen the CPC's capacity for governance and leadership to ensure that it will be able to guide the nation towards national renewal.

Today's domestic and international challenges are hugely complex and daunting. The CPC must demonstrate great political strength and competence to effectively lead such a large socialist country of more than 1.3 billion people steadily forward. Eight pillars of capacity building for governance and leadership were outlined at the 19th CPC National Congress, aimed at encouraging innovation, building cohesion, and improving effectiveness.

We must unlock potential for innovation. To govern well, the CPC must draw on its abilities to innovate, since we need new approaches to address the risks and challenges ahead. We must be eager to learn, sharpen leadership skills, promote reform and innovation, and build a Marxist party that values continuous learning. We must be able to think strategically, innovatively, and dialectically. We must promote the rule of law. And we must adopt a mentality against the worst-case scenario. By fostering an enterprising and inquiring frame of mind practical projects can be dealt with in new ways; the Internet and IT can be used more widely to improve effectiveness. By harnessing the power of innovation, we will be better positioned to respond to contemporary realities. The CPC will be stronger to pursue the dream of national renewal.

We must forge cohesion. The CPC's strength comes from the people, and only when there is cohesion is there strength. We need the support of the people to accomplish new tasks in a new era in response to new realities. Through innovative mechanisms we can engage better with the public, and promote greater political participation by civil society, such as trade unions, the Youth League, and the All-China Women's Federation. This will strengthen their role as progressive organizations acting as a bridge between the CPC and

the public to better represent them, and mobilize popular support for our common cause.

We must improve effectiveness. CPC effectiveness demonstrates its vigor and dynamism. Only by being more effective, can we overcome risks and challenges, and lead the people from victory to victory. Sustainable social and economic development, relying on the law, detailed program implementation, and risk control all require better skills and expertise. Perseverance, courage and meticulousness are key.

WITH HARD WORK WILL COME A BETTER FUTURE

The Party is the key to national renewal. Today, we are closer than ever before to realizing this great dream, and we are more confident than ever that we can make it happen. At this critical juncture, we cannot afford to pause nor falter. This is no time to relax or evade difficulties. We must now stay focused, and forge ahead. We have a huge task before us and we must be prepared for persistent hard work to build our better future. All Party members must put their shoulders to the wheel to move our great cause forward.

We must seize the moment. At this time, we have an unprecedented historic opportunity to realize socialist modernization. A golden era has dawned for us as a country, as a people and as individuals. History's baton has been passed to our generation, and we should rise to the occasion with courage, stamina, and strength to create a better future.

Assume responsibility. The courage to assume responsibility and the resolve to achieve real results are key to the victory for socialism with Chinese characteristics in this new era. Officials at all levels must demonstrate these qualities which are also important for assessing their performance. Those in leading positions must have the courage to step forward and take charge when difficulties or crises arise. They should not be tempted by fame or fortune. Instead, they should remember their responsibility and mission, take the initiative, be positive and forward-looking to set an example for others.

Cohesion and unity will overcome challenges, no matter how daunting. As the saying goes, if we work as one, we can move a mountain. Building socialism with Chinese characteristics in the new era is an ambitious undertaking that requires the efforts of millions of people. All Party members must consciously safeguard unity within the Party, and maintain close ties with the people. The CPC must build national cohesion and unity among all ethnic groups as well as among all Chinese nationals, including the overseas Chinese. We need the broadest possible unity to realize national rejuvenation.

Hard work for real results. Building a high tower starts from the ground up. Without hard work and perseverance we will accomplish nothing. Many generations have fought and worked to make China what it is today, a nation which has stood up, moved into prosperity and is now standing strong. Words and promises are not enough. We must move forward, one step at a time. All leaders must take on their responsibilities, be strong, dedicated, practical and effective.

As we enter this new era, we are embarking on a new journey which demands fresh thinking and a new spirit. As long as the CPC is clean and strong, always stands with the people and works in their interest, it will able to guide our nation's voyage across turbulent waters towards our great dream.

Effective measures for Party discipline enforcement since 2012

1. Integrate ethics education with institution building;

2. Combine a general mission-driven approach with specific issues;

3. Focus on a small number of key problems but also don't forget the others;

4. Ensure both effective control and accountability;

5. Combine strict supervision with empathy and trust; and

6. Combine internal Party oversight with public scrutiny.

Rules and regulations that have been promulgated or amended since 2012

- Eight Rules on Improving Official Conduct and Ties with the Public, December 2012;

- Guidelines on Duty Reassignment for Public Officials Whose Spouses Have Emigrated Overseas, February 2014;

- CPC Code of Ethics, October 2015;

- CPC Disciplinary Action Regulations, October 2015;

- CPC Accountability Regulations, July 2016;

- Code of Conduct for Intra-Party Political Activities in the New Era, October 2016;

- CPC Intra-Party Supervision Regulations, October 2017;

- CPC Disciplinary Inspection Regulations, July 2017; and

- CPC Transparency Regulations (Provisional), December 2017.

Four challenging requirements

In his opening remarks at a workshop on implementing the principles of the 19th CPC National Congress on January 5, 2018, General Secretary Xi Jinping emphasized the importance of fulfilling four challenging requirements. These are: (a) to remember lessons from history and not let past glories blind one to potential perils, and to retain the enthusiasm and drive of the earliest days; (b) always be humble and prudent in the exercise of power; (c) enforce strict discipline, stamp out corruption, and eliminate wastefulness; and (d) be responsive to changing circumstances and follow the will of the people.

General Secretary Xi Jinping's comments on Party conduct

In December 2017 General Secretary Xi Jinping made important comments on a Xinhua News Agency article entitled "Guard Against New Kinds of Formalities and Red Tape". He pointed out that the ills highlighted in the article, especially those related to preferring form over substance, red tape, self-indulgence, and wastefulness, are stubbornly recurring issues not anything new, so countering them was never going to end.

Party committees and governments at all levels should discuss and evaluate the conduct of public officials to identify shortcomings, especially problems long on promise but short on delivery. Strict steps should be taken to get real results. Officials at all levels should set good examples to create a positive environment. The forthcoming education drive to reaffirm our founding mission will also focus on battling this persistent obsession with show over substance.

The "Four-level" scale for oversight and enforcement

The CPC Intra-Party Supervision Regulations state that discipline enforcement must first and foremost focus on internal Party discipline. A comprehensive disciplinary framework consists of four types of actions, ranging from the most widely applicable to the least, and classified into varying degrees of severity. Since moral deterioration occurs over time, from light to severe, corresponding actions also progress from light to severe:

1. Frequent sessions for criticism and self-criticism, face-to-face talks, and warning letters, which serve as habitual reminders to guard against unethical conduct;

2. Censures or reprimands for minor infractions, together with possible reassignment of duties, which involve the greatest number of officials;

3. Demotions which are a major disciplinary action targeting a small number of officials; and

4. Criminal investigation which targets very few officials.

Eight pillars of capacity building for governance and leadership

1. Embrace continuous learning and study, create an atmosphere in which learning and practice are encouraged, and build a Marxist party that values continuous learning and a country that encourages continuous learning;

2. Sharpen leadership skills, improve the ability to think strategically, innovatively and dialectically, promote the rule of law, and maintain a mentality against the worst-case scenario; employ rigorous methods to develop guidelines and policies and implement them properly so as to ensure the CPC's role of leadership and coordination in all areas;

3. Further stimulate a spirit of enterprise and openness so as to promote reform and innovation, be willing to apply new ideas to practical projects, and become skilled in the use of the Internet and information technology;

4. Become more proficient in development planning that is systematic, fact-based and sustainable, be prepared to apply new development theories that break new ground;

5. Learn how to better rely on the rule of law to govern, speed up developing and refining a system of rules and regulations that cover all aspects of CPC leadership and Party building, so that it can better direct national government bodies;

6. Learn new ways to engage with the public, and promote greater political participation by civil socity, such as progressive organizations like trade unions, the Youth League, and the All-China Women's Federation, so they will act as a better bridge between the Party and the people, and mobilize them to support our common cause;

7. Become better at carrying out programs and projects on the ground by being resourceful and producing real results, acting quickly, with perseverance, meticulousness and courage when difficulties arise; and

8. Improve skills to manage risk, refine risk prevention and control mechanisms, learn how to resolve complex issues, and always keep the initiative.